A SUBSTITUTE FOR HOLINESS OR, ANTINOMIANISM REVIVED

Daniel Steele

WIPF & STOCK · Eugene, Oregon

Wipf and Stock Publishers
199 W 8th Ave, Suite 3
Eugene, OR 97401

A Substitute for Holiness Or, Antinomianism Revived
By Steele, Daniel
ISBN 13: 978-1-4982-9440-9
Publication date 5/30/2016
Previously published by McDonald, Gill & Co., 1889

A SUBSTITUTE FOR HOLINESS

OR,

ANTINOMIANISM REVIVED;

OR,

THE THEOLOGY OF THE SO-CALLED PLYMOUTH BRETHREN EXAMINED AND REFUTED.

BY

DANIEL STEELE, S.T.D.

RECENT PROFESSOR OF DIDACTIC THEOLOGY IN BOSTON UNIVERSITY

Author of "Commentaries on Leviticus, Numbers, and Joshua," "Love Enthroned," "Mile-Stone Papers," "Half Hours with St. Paul," "Defense of Christian Perfection," "The Gospel of the Comforter," "Jesus Exultant," etc.

THIRD EDITION, WITH INDEX

AND

APPENDIX BY THE LATE REV. C. MUNGER.

NOTE TO THE SECOND EDITION.

A NEW EDITION being called for, the opportunity is seized for adding in a valuable Appendix much new matter, not the least of which is the last earthly work of the late and sainted Rev. Charles Munger, D.D. Most opportunely and clearly does he show the novelty and unscripturalness of the premillennialism now so rampant among the Plymouth Brethren, and the manifoldly larger number of their conscious or unconscious sympathizers within all the churches.

Of great and welcome force are the wise words of the celebrated Rev. Robert Hall, down to Spurgeon confessedly the most eminent of England's Baptist ministers.

To the end that their young ministers may be promptly and properly indoctrinated, the Methodist Church of Canada has honored this little work with a place in its Course of Study for Travelling Preachers, an act which marks the doctrinal alertness of that body.

In a slightly modified form it has also been translated and published in India, as an antidote to the dangerous and indigenous teachings mentioned by Bishop Taylor on page 161.

The voluminous Indexes, both to Subjects and Texts, will be appreciated.

W. F. S.

"*Ques.* 19. What is Antinomianism?
Ans. The doctrine which makes void the law through faith."
Minutes of Wesley's First Conference, 1744.

"I dread every approach to antinomianism; I have seen the fruit of it over the three Kingdoms."
J. Wesley, 24 years later, 1768, letter 193.

"The great hindrance to the inward work of God is Antinomianism, wherever it breaks in. I am glad you are aware of it."
J. Wesley, 45 years later, 1789, letter 515.

"Antinomianism is a monster which can live only in darkness; bring light on it, and it expires."
Robert Hall, Pastor of the Baptist Church, Bristol.

CONTENTS.

	PAGE.
INTRODUCTION	5
PREFACE	23

CHAPTER I.
ANTINOMIANISM DEFINED 31

CHAPTER II.
ANTINOMIANISM.—HISTORICAL SKETCH . . 37

CHAPTER III.
THE PLYMOUTH BRETHREN 52

CHAPTER IV.
THE PLYMOUTH BRETHREN (*Continued*) . . 77

CHAPTER V.
ANTINOMIAN FAITH 100

CHAPTER VI.
THE PLYMOUTH VIEW OF THE ATONEMENT . 121

CHAPTER VII.
ETERNAL LIFE NON-FORFEITABLE . . . 132

CONTENTS.

CHAPTER VIII.
Holiness Imputed 148

CHAPTER IX.
Plymouth Eschatology, or Last Things . 162

CHAPTER X.
The Prophetic Conference Reviewed . . 193

CHAPTER XI.
Difficulties of Literalism 204

CHAPTER XII.
Predestinarian Basis 214

CHAPTER XIII.
Exegetical Absurdities 223

CHAPTER XIV.
Difficulties in the Thousand Years . . 235

CHAPTER XV.
The Church not the Kingdom 246

CHAPTER XVI.
Elect Number of the Gentiles . . . 256
Appendix 271

INTRODUCTION.

THE arguments of this book are directed, mainly, against the doctrines inculcated by the so-called *Plymouth Brethren*. We shall attempt little more, in this introduction which we are asked to write, than to answer the question, "Who are the *Plymouth Brethren?*"

They are a sect (if it be proper to call those a sect who repudiate all sects) popularly known as "Darbyites," "Brethren," "Plymouth Brethren," etc. They originated in England nearly sixty years ago, under the leadership of Mr. John Darby.

Mr. Darby was born in England, of wealthy parents. He was educated for the law, and commenced its practice. But his subsequent conversion changed his whole course of life. He was impressed that it was his duty to enter the ministry. His father, learning of his purpose, became violently opposed to it, and not being able to dissuade him from it, actually disinherited him. But a wealthy uncle adopted him, and at his decease left him an ample fortune.

Mr. Darby having finished his theological studies, was ordained, and admitted to the ministry of the Established Church. But he did not long continue in fellowship with that church. Not being able to understand the doctrine of apostolic succession, he rejected it, and withdrew from the Establishment and denounced it as an illegitimate church.

Having severed his connection with what he regarded an apostate church, he went in search of the true one, not doubting as yet but what such a church could be found. But Mr. Darby never found his ideal church.

Such as were of his way of thinking were urged to band themselves together and wait until Christ should make His personal advent, which they confidently anticipated would speedily occur. The first band of this faith was formed in Ireland. But it was in Plymouth, England, that the Brethren met with the greatest favor. Here their members soon numbered some fifteen hundred. So marked was their success in Plymouth, that they were called "Plymouth Brethren." It is proper to say, that they have never assumed this name, nor, in fact, any other, except "Brethren." Nor do we know that they seriously object to it.

Great success attended the labors of the "Brethren," and bands were formed in London, Exeter, and several other places. Many persons of wealth united with them, and contributed considerable sums of money to aid in spreading the new faith.

About this time they established their first periodical, entitled the *Christian Witness*, Mr. Darby being its chief contributor.

It was not long before their violent attacks on the church drew upon them the opposition of the English clergy. And so well directed and ably conducted was that opposition, that the spread of the new faith was not only seriously checked, but their numbers were greatly reduced.

In 1838, or near that time, Mr. Darby left England for the Continent. He first visited Paris, where he remained for a time, without seeing much fruit of his labor. But in Switzerland, which he next visited, he found a more inviting field.

Some time before Mr. Darby's visit to Switzerland, the Wesleyan Methodists had commenced successful operations in Lausanne, and quite a number of the members of the State Church had withdrawn and united with them, creating no little stir among the people.

Among the new proselytes to Methodism were some who still held to the doctrine of predestination, and rejected the Wesleyan doctrine of Christian perfection. It was claimed that, under these circumstances, those who held the doctrine of predestination, and still adhered to the Methodists, had received but half the truth. These differences of religious opinion extended to the Methodists of Vevay, producing no little disturbance among the members there.

With the purpose of overthrowing the new faith, an influential member of the State Church at Lausanne, invited Mr. Darby to come there and fight the Methodists. He went, and by his preaching, and the publication of a book entitled, *The Doctrine of the Wesleyans Regarding Perfection, and their use of the Holy Scriptures,* he succeeded in so far bewildering the uninstructed people, that the greater part of them abandoned their faith, and either returned to the State Church, or united with the dissenters.

Mr. Darby seemed to have still more in his plan. He delivered a series of lectures on the prophecies, entitled, *Views Regarding the Actual Expectation of the Church, and the Prophecies which Establish it.* These lectures were largely attended, and produced a profound impression upon all classes. They were subsequently published in French, German, and English, and may be found in Mr. Darby's published works. In the estimation of the author, at least, they lifted the veil which had long covered the prophecies.

Mr. Darby's influence with the people is said to have been so great that the regular ministry was almost entirely ignored, and he became the accepted prophet. In fact, his publications had the effect to turn the people, as a whole, from the ministry.

It was his custom to administer the sacrament every Sabbath indiscriminately to churchmen and dissenters, which practice earned for him the reputation of being a large-hearted Christian, anxious to make the church one.

When Mr. Darby had sufficiently drawn the people to *himself*, he was prepared, it would seem, to make known to them his plans more fully. These were, to draw out of the State

Church its best members, and unite them with others, and so form a circle of perfectly free congregations, without any organization, and to make himself, it was claimed, the centre of the whole.

To accomplish this end, a series of "fly-sheets," or tracts, were issued at Geneva and Lausanne, which clearly revealed Mr. Darby's plan. In one of these tracts, entitled, "Apostacy of the Economy," he laid the axe at the root of the tree, leaving the whole Christian Church, so far as he was able, a shapeless wreck. In another tract, "On the Foundation of the Church," he attacked the Dissenters, denying the right to form a church. In still another, "Liberty to preach Jesus possessed of every Christian," he denied the existence of any priestly office in the church, except the universal priesthood of believers. The church having come to an end, the ordained ministry, or priesthood, went with it. No man, nor body of men. Mr. Darby claimed, had any right to such an office, and to assume any such right was proof of the corruption and ruin of the whole system. In another tract, entitled "The Promise of the Lord," based on Matt. xviii. 20, is given the *shibboleth* of the Darbyite gatherings. Finally, a tract entitled, "Schism" was issued, in which all who hesitated to take part in these gatherings were denominated, "Schismatics."

It will be seen at a glance that the work of demolition progressed with great rapidity The church is first demolished. Mr. Darby does not allow even a poor Dissenter to organize a new one, no matter how good it might be. Next, the Gospel ministry is swept away, and should any one set up a claim to such an office, he would give the clearest evidence of his corruption. In this way the world is left without a church and without a ministry; and the only substitute furnished is a few Darbyite gatherings, which are without form and without responsibility. From Switzerland they spread into France, and gathered, after a time, several congregations in Paris, Lyons, Marseilles, and other places. A French periodical was established for the propagation of their principles, and a kind of seminary was started for training Missionaries.

That secessions should occur where no organizations exist, and where all organizations are utterly repudiated, seems strange. But it was not possible for persons, who could readily accept such radical views as Mr. Darby enunciated, to be long held by them. This is pre-eminently true of the Plymouth Brethren.

A division soon took place under the leadership of Mr. B. W. Newton. It originated in England, but extended to the Continent. Mr. Newton, it is claimed, held with Irving that Christ was not sinless. This notion was earnestly repelled by most of the Darbyites, and the obnoxious Newton was formally expelled by Mr. Darby. We will not stop to inquire how Mr. Darby could have consistently expelled a man from his society, when he ignored and utterly repudiated all organizations. The Newton heresy extended into Vevay, where considerable trouble followed. The "Brethren" there split into two factions; and this was soon followed by several other societies.

Another division took place in England, in which Mr. George Müller, of Bristol, was the most prominent actor. Other divisions have taken place.

In America there are several schools of the Plymouth Brethren. Mr. Darby is utterly ignored by some of them. While the old man was still living they went so far as to represent him as a second "Diotrephes, who loveth to have the pre-eminence" (3 John 9). They insinuated that Mr. Darby, the father of them all, had very far fallen from original Darbyism; at least, this would be naturally inferred from the manner in which they treated him. We have in Boston, and other places, two classes, or schools, of the Plymouth Brethren.

INTRODUCTION. 15

The religious views of the Plymouth Brethren are fully set forth, by Dr. Steele, in the following pages. They are Antinomians of the straitest sect. Everything but pure Darbyism belongs to this world. There is nobody right but themselves. The church is fallen, and cannot be reformed, and our only duty is to go out of her. Anything which looks like church prosperity is, with the Plymouth Brethren, a delusion. "The year-books of Christianity," says Mr. Darby, "are the year-books of hell."

One of their writers, speaking of the church, says: "It is a corrupt mysterious mixture, a spiritual malformation, the master-piece of Satan, the corrupter of the truth of God." "It is that thing which Satan has made of professing Christianity. It is worse, by far, than Judaism; worse by far than all the darkest forms of Paganism,"

The *New Birth*, with a Plymouth Brother, is not a change of our old nature, but the formation of a new man who is distinguished in all things from the old — has his own customs, wishes, aims, feelings and necessities — and these are spiritual, heavenly and Divine. The old man, instead of being absolutely crucified and put to death, *was* only crucified *in* Christ eighteen hundred years ago, while, in fact, he actually lives and grows, often worse and worse, to the end of life. In response to a question we once put to Mr. Darby, he said, his nature or old man, had been growing worse and worse ever since he had believed in Christ. But he paid no attention to that, as he was saved *in* Christ and had nothing to do with the old man — the carnal mind. One of their number puts it thus: "The believer's state can never correspond with his standing." The seventh and eighth of Romans exist in the same heart, and at the same time.

Mr. McIntosh, their most venerated authority, says: "Flesh is flesh, nor can it ever be made aught else but flesh. The Holy Ghost did not come down on the day of Pentecost to improve nature, or do away the fact of its incurable evil, but to baptize believers into one body, and connect them with their living head in Heaven."

Perfect holiness, with the Brethren, is one and the same with justification. It is, or was, a finished work of God. It is in no sense personal in ourselves, but *in* Christ, and accomplished when He died on the cross. It can never be diminished nor increased. No sin committed by a justified person can in the least affect his justification. The soul's standing must ever remain as pure as Christ Himself. He may get drunk like Noah, commit murder and adultery like David, curse like Peter, or lie like Ananias and Sapphira, and his *standing* is no more affected by it than was Stephen's when under a shower of stones, with his face shining like that of an angel.

One of their writers gives the following description of a good man:—

"The good man feels that when he is presenting to God his prayer and his praises and other holy things, that many vain and foolish thoughts often come unbidden, as the unclean fowls came down upon the sacrifice which Abraham had laid in order to be offered to God (Gen. xv. 11); and he feels that his sacrifice is sadly spoiled; and he asks, 'Can the pure God accept such impure sacrifices as I now bring and lay on His altar?' There is so much of self and sin in our holiest things that our very tears need washing, and our very repentance towards God needs to be repented of. In each of our hearts there is a fountain of black, filthy waters; and when we think we are about to present a gift pure and clean to God, the stream bursts forth, and the gifts we thought would be so clean and pure are besmeared with vile effusions of our own corrupt heart. And we often think that Satan empties much of the horrible filth of hell into our hearts, making each of them into a sewer for the foul waters of the abyss of despair to run through."

Can anything worse than this be said of the most wicked man living? Satan can do no worse than to empty the "horrible filth of hell into his heart," and make him a "sewer for the foul waters of the abyss of despair to run through." This is the best thing the Gospel of the Plymouth Brethren can do for poor, fallen, human nature. And yet, strange to say, this same man, who is filled with the "horrible filth of hell," and is a "sewer for the foul waters of the abyss of despair to run through," is, at the same time, pure as Christ is pure. Here are his words:—

"He who is our Great High Priest before God is pure without a stain. God sees Him as such, and He stands for us who are His people, and we are accepted in Him. His holiness is ours by imputation. Standing *in Him* we are in the sight of God, holy as Christ is holy, and pure as Christ is pure. God looks at our representative, and He sees us in Him. We are complete in Him who is our spotless and glorious Head."

Here is full-fledged Antinomianism.

The Plymouth Brethren profess to have no creed but the Bible. They condemn all who avow a creed, as putting human opinions in the place of the Word of God. And yet they seem to have a well-defined creed, and put it forth with great persistency.* They denounce all commentaries on the Scriptures as misleading; and yet Mr. Darby has written commentaries quite extensively on the Bible, to say nothing of Mr. McIntosh, whom they regard as nearly, if not quite, inspired.

They do not labor for sinners, but for the members of the various churches, as if they were in more peril than the outside world. They may be seen around revival meetings with tracts in hand, containing antagonistic sentiments, to be placed in the hands of new converts, for the purpose of mystifying them, and drawing them away from Christ and salvation,

---

* To find out whether they were a sect, that is, a fragment cutting itself off from the general Church of Christ, the author of this volume once asked Mr. Darby whether he would be permitted to partake of the Lord's Supper with them, if he should present himself. Mr. Darby replied that he would be allowed to partake, provided he should correctly answer certain doctrinal questions. The other "Brethren" present strongly dissented from such liberty, and intimated close communion. Hence, while denouncing all schisms and sects, they are a sect of the straightest and most exclusive kind.

and in this way make proselytes to their faith, not from the world, but from the churches.

We bid all a hearty God-speed who are working for the salvation of souls. And did we believe that souls are made better by accepting the dogmas of the Plymouth Brethren, we should most heartily say: "Go on, and the Lord bless you." But so far as we can see, their teachings are evil, and only evil. It makes chaos of order, and deceives souls by assuring them that they are *in* Christ, while they are full of corruption.

Dr. Steele has done a valuable service for all the churches; for Plymouthism successful, means the churches depleted. While they may hold some views in common with some of the evangelical churches, their main purpose is to undermine the churches, and foster a spirit that would lay waste every church in Christendom. We firmly believe that this book will greatly aid in arresting this growing tide of error.

W. McDonald.

PREFACE.

It is no secret that the author of this book believes in a large Gospel, an evangel co-extensive with the present needs of the depraved offspring of Adam; yea, more: he believes that where sin hath abounded, grace doth here and now much more abound to those believers who insist that Christ is a perfect Saviour from inbred sin, through the efficacy of His blood, in procuring the indwelling Comforter and Sanctifier. He unhesitatingly proclaims and testifies to all the world that Jesus Christ can make clean the inside, as well as the outside of His vessels unto honor; that heart-purity is real and inwrought, and not a stainless robe, concealing unspeakable moral filthiness and leprosy. He believes with St. John against the Gnostics, that if any man asserts that he has by nature no defiling taint of depravity, no bent toward acts of sin, and hence, that he does not need the blood of atonement, that he is self-deceived, and the truth is not in him; but if he will confess his lost condition, God is faithful and just, not only to forgive, but also to cleanse from all sin, "actual and original" (Bengel). He is bold to assert that we are living in the days when Ezekiel's prophecy is fulfilled: "I will sprinkle clean water upon you, and ye shall be clean; from ALL your filthiness and from ALL your idols I will cleanse you; I will put my spirit within you, and cause you to walk in my statutes,"— a case of evangelical legalism,—"and ye shall keep my judgments, and do them. I will also save you from all your uncleannesses"; and in the days when the words of Jehovah, by the lips of Moses, are verified in the experience of a multitude of believers: "The Lord thy God will circumcise thy heart, and the heart of thy seed, to love the Lord thy God with all thine heart, and with all thy soul, that thou mayest live." He finds St. Paul's inspired unfoldings of the Gospel germs, dropped by Christ, to be the exact fulfilment and realization of these predictions, when the Apostle asserts that "our old man is crucified with him" — that is, in the same manner, and with as deadly an effect — "that the body of sin might be destroyed" — "put out of existence" (Meyer); so that every advanced believer may truthfully assert, "it is no longer I that live" (*R. V. Am. Committee*).

He is confident that the law of the Spirit of life in Christ Jesus does now "make us free from the law of sin and death," although it does not, this side of the grave, deliver us from errors, ignorances, and such innocent infirmities as St. Paul gloried in without detriment to his saintly character. Believing, as the author is not ashamed to confess with tongue and type and telegraph and telephone, in a genuine CHRISTIAN PERFECTION — a Scriptural term which cannot be used " without raising the pity or indignation of one-half of the religious world, some making it the subject of their pious sneers " — he views with sorrow the resurrection of that spurious perfection which wrought disastrous effects in past generations, consisting in an imaginary perfect and inalienable standing in Christ wholly independent of moral conduct and character, the outcome of which must inevitably be, in many cases, the rejection of God's law as the rule of life, and a sad lowering of the standard of Christian morality. It is an evil omen when Christian teachers make eloquent pleas for the flesh, and fallaciously construct ingenious Scriptural arguments for indwelling sin. So long as the believer dwells in the body, such preaching, instead of inspiring unspeakable abhorrence for sin, deadens men's sensibility to its dreadful nature and leads them " to speak of the corruptions of their hearts in as unaffected and airy a manner, as if they talked of freckles upon their faces, and to run down their sinful nature only to apologize for their sinful practices; or to appear great proficients in self-knowledge, and court the praise due to genuine humility."

We have noted the fact that a school of popular evangelists have espoused the doctrines which lie at the base of Antinomianism, and that they are zealously inculcating these peculiar tenets in Young Men's Christian Associations and summer schools. We have done what we could, by articles in our Christian periodicals, to warn the public of the certain evil results which will ensue when these doctrines descend from the few Christian teachers who, by well-established Christian habits, are fortified against their pernicious tendency, to the multitudes of weak believers who may be ensnared to their moral ruin by the pleasing doctrine that one act of faith in Christ secures a perpetual exemption from condemnation, and a lifelong license for walking in the flesh.

Some teachers of this doctrine may live in

harmony with the purest ethical precepts of Christ, under what Joseph Cook calls "hereditary momentum," and a personal experience of salvation in former years, before embracing their present theological errors. But what will be the legitimate fruit in those who give full credence to a theoretical error lying so near to conduct and character, and who are without the safeguards of which we have just spoken?

From our knowledge of the human heart we forebode many shipwrecks of moral character. Men generally live below their creeds; few rise above them. Illustration: A preacher riding on top of an omnibus, in London, addressed words of reproof to a tipsy man by his side, who was using very improper language, and warned him as a transgressor of the law of God. "Oh," said the man, "it is not by works, it is by faith, and I believe in Jesus Christ, and of course I shall be saved." Here is a man, a sample of myriads, who are living in wilful sin, dreaming of final salvation on the ground of a barren, fruitless, speculative belief that Jesus Christ died for their salvation, a faith which no more reforms the conduct and transforms the character, than faith in the existence of the sea-serpent.

The fatal mistake is in ignoring the Scriptural test of saving faith, evangelical works. It is true that the penitent believer seeking the pardon of sin is justified by faith only. But it is also true that in the day of Judgment the same person will be judged by works only, works which attest the genuineness of his faith (Jer. xvii. 10; xxxii. 19; Ezek. vii. 3, 27; xviii. 20, 30; 1 Cor. iii. 8, 13–15; 2 Cor. v. 10; Gal. vi. 5–8; especially Matt. xxv. 31–46).

It is due to the Christian public that I should acknowledge my sense of incompetency for the proper handling of this subject. I have long waited for some eminent theologian to lift up his voice in refutation of a system of error which is industriously promoted by persons whose zeal is worthy of a better cause. At length I have yielded to the importunity of many Christian men to expose the character and tendencies of that system of doctrines against which this book is prayerfully directed.

I have made a free use of that great armory of weapons — "Fletcher's Checks to Antinomianism." Sometimes I have quoted sentences unchanged, noting them with quotation marks. But frequently these marks could not be used by reason of the alterations which I have made, either to abridge, to modernize, or to eliminate some personal allusion.

In my quotations from the writings of the Plymouth Brethren and their sympathizers, I have endeavored to give the exact idea of the writer as gathered from the context.

Whoever of my Christian friends may be grieved, I trust that the great day will reveal that truth has not been wounded, but rather cleared of errors and set forth in the robes of her native beauty.

ANTINOMIANISM REVIVED.

CHAPTER I.

ANTINOMIANISM DEFINED.

REV. J. FLETCHER says, "An Antinomian is a professor of Christianity, who is *antinomos*, against the law of Christ, as well as against the law of Moses. He allows Christ's law to be a rule of life, but not a rule of judgment for believers, and thus he destroys that law at a stroke, as a law; it being evident that a rule by the personal observance or non-observance of which Christ's subjects can never be acquitted or condemned, is not a law for them. Hence he asserts that Christians shall no more be justified before God by their personal obedience to the law of Christ, than by their personal obedience to the ceremonial law of Moses. Nay, he believes that the best of Christians perpetually break Christ's law; that nobody ever kept it but Christ Himself; and that we shall be justified or condemned before God, in the great day, not as we shall personally be found to have finally kept or broken Christ's law, but as God shall be found to have, before the foundation of the world, arbitrarily laid, or not laid, to our account, the merit of Christ's keeping His own law. Thus he hopes to stand in the great day, merely by what he calls 'Christ's imputed righteousness'; excluding with abhorrence, from our final justification, the evangelical worthiness of our own personal, sincere obedience of repentance and faith, — a precious obedience this which he calls 'dung, dross, and filthy rags' just as if it were the insincere obedience of self-righteous pride, and Pharisaic hypocrisy. Nevertheless, though he thus excludes the evangelical, derived worthiness of the works of faith, from our eternal justification and salvation, he himself does good works, if he is in other respects a good man. Nay, in this case, he piques himself on doing them, thinking he is peculiarly obliged to make people believe that, immoral as his sentiments are, they draw after them the greatest benevolence and the strictest morality." This reminds us of the testimony of a Universalist woman, "That she had come three miles to attend this prayer-meeting, so as to show that the Universalists are as pious as the Orthodox."

But there are multitudes carelessly following the stream of corrupt nature who are crying out, not against the unholiness, but against the "*legality*, of their wicked hearts, which still suggest that they must *do something*, in order to attain eternal life." They decry that evangelical legality which all true Christians are in love with — a cleaving to Christ by that kind of faith which works righteousness — a following Him as He went about doing good, and a showing by St. James' *works* that we have St. Paul's faith.

The consistent Antinomian — that is, one whose practice accords with his theory — is loud in his proclamation of a finished eternal salvation, the blotting out of his sins, past, present and future, on the Cross eighteen hundred years ago, without respect to his own conduct, character, or works. His salvation is so finished that no sins can ever blot his name out of the Book of Life. He thinks that the Son of God magnified the law that we might vilify it; that He made it honorable, that we might make it contemptible; that He came to fulfil it, that we might be discharged from fulfilling it, according to our capacity. He has no sympathy with David's confession: "I love Thy commandments above gold and precious stones: I will always keep Thy law, yea, forever and ever: I will walk at LIBERTY, for I seek Thy precepts."

ANTINOMIANISM DEFINED.

In short, the creed of the Antinomian is this: I was justified when Christ died, and my faith is simply a waking up to the fact that I have always been saved — a realization of what was done before I had any being; that a believer is not bound to mourn for sin, because it was pardoned before it was committed, and pardoned sin is no sin; that God does not see sin in believers, however great sins they commit; that by God's laying our iniquities upon Christ, He became as completely sinful as I, and I as completely righteous as Christ. Moreover, I believe that no sin can do a believer any ultimate harm, although it may temporarily interrupt communion with God. I must not do any duty for my own salvation. This is included in the new covenant, which is all of it a promise, having no condition on my part. It is a paid up, non-forfeitable, eternal-life insurance policy. Since the new covenant is not properly made with us, but with Christ for us, the conditions, repentance, faith, and obedience, are not on our side, but on Christ's side, who repented, believed, and obeyed, in such a way as to relieve us from these unpleasant acts. Hence it is folly to search for inward marks of grace, and it is a fundamental error to make sanctification an indispensable evidence of justification — an error which dampens the joys of him who takes Christ for his sanctification, and plunges him into needless alarms and distresses."

CHAPTER II.

ANTINOMIANISM. — HISTORICAL SKETCH.

THEOLOGICAL errors move in cycles, sometimes of very long periods. They resemble those comets of unknown orbits which occasionally dash into our solar system; but they are not as harmless. Often they leave moral ruin in their track. Since all Christian truth is practical, and aims at the moral transformation of men, all negations of that truth are deleterious; they not only obscure the truth and obstruct its purifying effect, but they positively corrupt and destroy souls. This is specially true of errors which release men from obligation to the law of God. After St. Paul had demonstrated the impossibility of justification by works compensative for sin, and had established the doctrine of justification through a faith in Christ which works by love and purifies the heart, there started up a class of teachers who drew from Paul's teachings the fallacious inference that the law of God is abolished in the case of the believer, who is henceforth delivered from its authority as the rule of life. Hence they became, what Luther first styled, Antinomians (Greek *anti*, against, and *nomos*, law). We infer from Rom. iii. 8, 31; vi. 1; Eph. v. 6; 2 Peter ii. 18, 19, and James ii. 17–26, in which warnings are given against a perversion of the truth as an excuse for licentiousness, that Antinomianism, in its grosser form, found place in the primitive church. All along the history of the Church, a revival of the cardinal doctrine of justification, by faith only, has been followed by a resurrection of Antinomianism, which Wesley defines as " the doctrine which makes void the law through faith." Those who aver that ultra-Calvinism is the invariable antecedent of Antinomianism, would be unwilling to accept the necessary inference that the apostle to the Gentiles was an ultra-Calvinist; yet it is true that the doctrines of Calvinism can be logically pushed to that conclusion. It is also true that other forms of doctrine which emphasize faith in Jesus Christ, as the sole ground of acceptance with God, are more or less liable to have the tares of Antinomianism spring up in their field.

The root of this error lies in a false view of the mediatorial work of Christ, that He performs for men the obedience which they ought to perform, and that God can justly demand nothing further from the delinquents. It is claimed that Christ's perfect virtues are reckoned to the believer in such a way as to excuse him for their absence; His chastity compensating for the absence of that moral quality in the believer. Hence, adultery and murder in King David, being compensated by the purity and benevolence of Jesus imputed to him in the mind of God, did not mar David's standing as righteous before God.

Theologians who state the doctrine of the atonement with proper safeguards, are careful to limit its vicarious efficacy to the *passive* obedience of the Son of God, His sufferings and death. His *active* obedience constitutes no part of His substitutional work. The germ of Antinomianism is found in the inclusion of the latter in the atonement. It is true that the God-man was actively obedient to the Father's will, but this obedience was personal, and not mediatorial. Hence, every one justified through faith in the shed blood of Christ, is under obligation to render personal obedience to God's law. In this respect Jesus cannot be his proxy or representative.

Says Bishop Hopkins: "Though Christ's bearing the punishment of the law by death does exempt us from suffering, yet His obeying of the law does not excuse obedience to the law. He obeyed the law as a covenant of works — we only as a rule of righteousness."

It should be said that the Gnostic sects were

Antinomian on other grounds. They held that their spiritual natures could not contract moral pollution, whatever their moral conduct might be, sin inhering only in matter. As a piece of gold retains its purity while encompassed by the filth of the swine-sty, so the soul keeps pure amid the grossest sins. This species of Antinomianism was not limited to those who professed faith in Christ. It was adopted by all who held that all evil inheres in uncreated matter.

Modern Universalism is only another form of Antinomianism. It is the expectation of salvation through Christ, without obedience to either the law or the Gospel.

Christianity was very early disfigured by antinomianism, a doctrinal and practical error which opposes itself to God's law even in the evangelical form in which it was defined by His adorable Son, " Thou shalt love God with all thy heart, and thy neighbor as thyself." This had been the burden of Christ's preaching, with the hint that His own life was to be given, as a ransom for many, and to secure grace to enable them to fulfil God's law. The apostles, by precept and example, powerfully enforced their Lord's doctrine and practice. Their lives are true copies of their exhortations. It is hard to say which excite men most to believe and obey, their seraphic sermons or their saintly lives. Success crowned their labors. Both Judaism and paganism heard the thunder of their words of faith and fell prostrate beneath the lightning of their works of love. But before all is lost, Satan hastens to " transform himself into an angel of light." In this disguise he instills speculative faith, instead of a saving faith which works by love, purifies the heart, and overcomes the world; he pleads for loose living, puts the badge of contempt upon the daily cross, and gets multitudes of Laodiceans and Gnostics into his snare. Sad and sure is the result. Genuine works of faith are neglected; idle works of men's invention are substituted for those of God's commandments; and fallen churches, gliding downward through the smooth way of antinomianism, return to the covert way of Phariseeism, or to the broad way of infidelity.

Such was the distressing outlook upon the church when Luther arose. True faith was dethroned by superstitious fancy, and works were will nigh choked by the thorns of this baneful error. Luther swung the sharp scythe of reform over northern Europe, and he might have mowed a broad swath through Italy and Rome itself, if he had not at the same time scattered the dragons teeth of antinomianism, which sprang up around his German home an army of armed men. The balance of evangelical precepts had not been preserved in preaching the forgiveness of sins by faith only, without adding that this faith is genuine only when it buds, blossoms, and bears the fruitage of holy character.

Our Lord's sermon upon the Mount, was explained away, and St. James' Epistle was wished out of the Bible as an "epistle of straw," and not of the precious stones of Gospel truth. The practicable *law of Christ*, styled the law of liberty, because of the ease with which it could be kept by a regenerate soul entirely sanctified through the indwelling of the Holy Spirit, was perpetually confounded with that impracticable Christless *law of* Edenic innocence; and the avoidable penalties of the former were injudiciously represented as one with the dreadful curse of the latter, or with the abrogated ceremonies of Mosaism. Then the law of Christ demanding purity and love was publicly wedded to the devil, and poor bewildered Protestants were taught to defy and scoff at both. From such a seed-sowing the dreadful harvest waved over Germany. Lawless believers, under the name of Ana-Baptists, arose fancying themselves the dear elect people of God, reasoning thus: "First, the earth belongs to the saints, and, secondly, we are the saints." All things were theirs. They were complete in Christ, and absolutely sure of salvation by reason of their standing in Him. They went about in religious mobs to deliver people from *legal bondage*, and bring them into *Gospel liberty*, — a liberty to despise all laws, Divine and human, and to do every one what was right in his own eyes. Luther was alarmed and shocked. He hastened from his concealment in the castle of the Wartburg, to check a movement which was disgracing the Reformation. But the mischief was done; the thistle-seed had been broadcast over Germany. The only proper remedy he did not perseveringly apply: salvation, not by the merit of works, but by the works of faith, as a condition, and as a proof of its genuineness in the great day. Men are now justified from the guilt of sin by a work-producing faith. They will be justified in the day of judgment only on the testimony of faith-produced works.

Nevertheless, Luther learned wisdom enough to abandon the root of the mischief when he drew up, or, rather, indorsed, the Augsburg Confession, in which are these remarkable words: "We teach touching repentance, that those who have sinned after baptism may obtain the forgiveness of sins *as often as* they are converted," etc. Again: "We condemn the Anabaptists, who say that those who have been once justified can no more lose the Holy Spirit."

This antidote of Gospel truth, clearly and frequently enforced, might have stopped the spread of Antinomianism. But Luther did not insist upon it, vacillated, and sometimes seemed even to contradict it. When Calvin arose, though he seldom went the length of some of his followers in the next century in speculative Antinomianism, yet he laid excellent foundations for it in his un-Scriptural and unguarded doctrine of absolute decrees, and of the necessary, final perseverance of backsliding believers.

We have hinted that Antinomianism has had

its cycles in the history of the Church. Its full development, since the Reformation, is due to John Agricola (1492-1566), one of the early coadjutors of Luther, some of whose expressions, as to justification and the law, in the heat of his great controversy with Rome, were hasty, extravagant, and quite Antinomian. These utterances Agricola developed into a system so extreme, and so subversive of Christian morals, that he published in 1537 these words: "Art thou steeped in sin — an adulterer or a thief? If thou believest, thou art in salvation. All who follow Moses must go to the devil; to the gallows with Moses." This was the kind of tares sown in Luther's field by a professed friend. Luther attacked him violently, calling him a fanatic, and other hard names. After Agricola's death, Amsdorf and Otto advocated his doctrines, and maintained that good works are an obstacle to salvation. Similar sentiments were preached in England in the days of Oliver Cromwell. But it remained for Dr. Crisp, (1600–1642), a rector of the Church of England, to give this error its full development in Anglican theology, from the seed-corn of high Calvinism. The following sentiments abound in his sermons: "The law is cruel and tyrannical, requiring what is naturally impossible." "The sins of the elect were so imputed to Christ, as that, though He did not commit them, yet they became actually His transgressions, and ceased to be theirs. The feelings of conscience which tell them that sin is theirs, arise from a want of knowing the truth. It is but the voice of a lying spirit in the hearts of believers that saith they have yet sin wasting their conscience, and lying as a burden too heavy for them to bear. Christ's righteousness is so imputed to the elect, that they, ceasing to be sinners, are as righteous as He was, and all that He was. An elect person is not in a condemned state while an unbeliever; and should he happen to die before God calls him to believe, he would not be lost.

Repentance and confession of sin are not necessary to forgiveness. A believer may certainly conclude before confession, yea, as soon as he hath committed sin, the interest he hath in Christ, and the love of Christ embracing him."

This doctrine completely destroys the distinction between right and wrong, and removes all motives to abstain from sin. It boasts in the perseverance of the saints, while it believes in no saint but one, that is, Jesus, and neglects to persevere. Several vigorous theologians opposed this baneful doctrine, the chief of whom were Baxter and Williams, who, after heroic efforts and no small suffering, finally triumphed.

The next revival of Antinomianism in the Church of England and among the dissenters, was in the eighteenth century and was met most courageously by John Wesley, the apostle of experimental godliness and of Christian perfection, and by the seraphic John Fletcher, whose writings, says Dr. Dollinger, "are the most important theological productions which issued from Protestanism in the latter part of the eighteenth century." His reasoning is cogent, his imagination vivid, his style clear and incisive, and the momentum of his arguments is so irresistible that he swept the field, driving Antinomianism out of England during, at least, two generations. His "Checks" stand to-day unanswered and unanswerable. No man can read them with candor and continue to deny the obligation of believers to strict obedience to the law of God; that inwrought holiness is the requirement of the Gospel, and that there is no sharp contrast between it and the law.

A thorough study of these "Checks," by the ministry in our times, would wonderfully stimulate their spiritual life, tone up their theology, and furnish them with the weapons for the conflict with the cycle of Antinomian error which is now upon the Church.

The agency through which this heresy, entombed by Fletcher, has had its resurrection, is the so-called Plymouth Brethren, whose peculiar tenets will be described in the next chapter.

CHAPTER III.

THE PLYMOUTH BRETHREN.

WHAT are the Plymouth Brethren? This is a question which many people are asking. An old lady at Hamilton camp-meeting last year, hearing the writer comment on one of their doctrines, indignantly left the audience, exclaiming, "I have heard enough of the Plymouth Brethren and Beecher, too!" She was thinking of the Plymouth Church in Brooklyn.

The Plymouth Brethren originated in Dublin, Ireland, about the year 1830, and almost simultaneously in Plymouth, England. In the latter place they increased so rapidly that they once numbered 1,500. Hence they are called by outsiders Plymouth Brethren. Although they do not repudiate the word "Plymouth," they style themselves "The Brethren." Their leading mind, if not their original founder, who died a few years ago at an advanced age, is John Darby. Hence they are sometimes called Darbyites. The movement was at first a protest against ecclesiasticism, like that of George Fox, the first Quaker. Darby, a clergyman in the Church of England, renounced the Church, and assumed that all existing Church organizations are a detriment to Christianity, and obstructive of regeneration and the spiritual life. His little band of adherents claim to be a reproduction of the primitive disciples — the only genuine specimens on earth. They refuse to take any distinctive name, and disavow that they are a sect. They call themselves the Brethren, as if they were the only persons in the bonds of Christian brotherhood. They are all priests and all laymen. They insist that in Christianity there is no specially called and ordained ministerial order. In this they resemble the Friends; but, unlike them, they lay great stress upon ordinances, especially the Lord's Supper. This they celebrate alone by themselves every Lord's day, and it constitutes the chief part of their worship. To find out whether they are a sect, *i. e.*, a fragment cutting itself from the general Church of Christ, I once asked Mr. Darby whether I would be permitted to partake of the Lord's Supper with them if I should present myself. He replied that I would be allowed to partake, if I should correctly answer certain doctrinal questions. The other "Brethren" present strongly dissented from such liberality, and intimated close communion. Hence, while denouncing all schisms and sects, they are a sect of the straightest and most exclusive kind. They baptize by immersion only. Meetings for worship including only believers, are entirely different from meetings for preaching where the unregenerate are permitted to be present. They talk much about separation unto God, by which they mean abandonment of ecclesiastical organizations; and politics even, refraining from voting, insisting on deadness to the world and entire devotion to God, by going forth and preaching Christ wherever they can get a hearer. They make constant use of the Bible in private and in public, or, rather, of a certain line of texts, interpreted to sustain their peculiar tenets. Professing to rely only on the Word of God, you will find them all equipped with the commentaries of McIntosh, Darby, and others. To propagate their doctrines they scatter many tracts and small expository books.

Several years ago, D. L. Moody learned his method of Bible-study and Bible-readings from the English Plymouth Brethren. In his eagerness to attain a knowledge of the Bible, he made his first voyage to Europe, attracted by the fame of these students of the Holy Scriptures. Hence they claim him as a product of their system. In his earnest exhortation to converts to join some church, he certainly repudiates Plymouth come-out-ism, and he emphatically disclaims some of the theological tenets of the Brethren. Just how far he accords with them we do not know. He adopts their millenarianism, and preaches the personal reign of Christ on the earth as a substitute for the present agency of the Spirit and of preaching, which are regarded as inadequate for the successful evangelization of the whole world, and the reconstruction of society on a Christian basis. His declaration that the world is like a ship so hopelessly wrecked that it cannot be gotten off the rocks, but must be left to perish, while Christians rescue as many of the passengers as possible, is a pessimistic Plymouth idea.

In England the Brethren are quite numerous and influential. Some, as Tregelles, are very scholarly. Such men as Varley, Lord Radstock, Blackstone, and Muller, are either professed Brethren, or are in strong sympathy with them. They have missionaries in India whose disorganizing influence has given our Methodist missionaries some trouble, and has caused one secession, and the loss of several promising missionary stations. The Wesleyan Methodist societies in Lausanne and Vevay, in Switzerland, at one time suffered great loss through the bewilderment caused by the preaching of Mr. Darby against their doctrine of Christian perfection, and their use of the Holy Scriptures. The leaven of their doctrines has already spread widely in America, and their theological tenets are preached by leading ministers in Boston, New York, St. Louis, and other cities, while their theories of Church organization are rejected.

The Brethren, having no written creed and no Church discipline, are exposed to constant schisms, so that there are several sorts in England, and two sets in Boston at the present time who repudiate each other quite cordially. The anti-Darby party aver that the Holy Spirit has drawn the portrait of John Darby in 3 John 9, 10. But in the worst of their theological tenets they are quite generally agreed — their Antinomianism. We have heard Mr. Darby say that if any man had anything to do with the law of God, even to obey it, he was a sinner by that very act.

Their primal error seems to be in their conception of the Atonement. They teach that sin, as a kind of personality, was condemned on the cross of Christ and put away forever. Whose sins? Those of the believer. All his sins past, present, and future, are "judged" and swept away forever in the Atonement, and the believer is to have no more concern for his past or future sins, since they were blotted out eighteen hundred years ago. Here is their most mischievous tenet respecting faith and its relation to the Atonement and to eternal life: The first momentary act of faith renders the Atonement *eternally* available, and without any further conditions infallibly secures everlasting life. Hence the younger Dr. Tyng, in a recent sermon odorous of Plymouth, declared that in that act of faith the believer's "responsibility ends." This must mean that his probation ceases, his eternal salvation having been absolutely secured.

The object grasped by faith is not so much Jesus Christ, a present Saviour, as His finished work of condemning and putting away sin on the cross. "Faith grasps only past and finished acts." Intellectual assent to these historical facts, the atonement of Christ judging my sin, and His resurrection as the proof thereof, constitutes saving faith.

Their view of the Atonement is the old and exploded commercial theory — so much suffering by Christ equals so much suffering by the sinners saved by Christ. With this theory of the Atonement, they cannot proclaim its universality without teaching Universalism. So they make a distinction between the death of Christ for all, and the blood of Christ shed only for those who are, through faith, sprinkled and cleansed thereby. By this means God saves believers, and presents "an aspect of mercy" toward all mankind.

Their idea of justification is not that it is a present act, taking place in the mind of God in favor of the penitent believer, but it is a past, completed, wholesale transaction on Calvary ages ago. Faith puts a man into the realization of the fact that all his foreseen sins were then cast behind God's back forever, and that he has a through ticket to heaven.

In regeneration, the new man is created in the believer, and the old man remains with all his powers unchanged. Mr. Darby asserted to the writer that after more than fifty years of Christian experience he found the old man in himself worse than he was at his regeneration. Says McIntosh: "It is no part of the work of the Holy Spirit to improve human nature," — that seems to be past praying for, — but to make a brand-new man to dwell in the same body with the old man till physical death luckily comes and kills the old Adam who had successfully defied all power in heaven and earth effectually to crucify him. Henceforth the new man has the entire possession of the disembodied soul. How different this from a holiness bearing its heavenly fruit this side of the grave (Luke i. 74, 75; Rom. vi. 6, 19, 22; 2 Cor. vii. 2; 1 Thess. iii. 13; iv. 7; ii. 10; Heb. xii. 10, 14; Col. ii. 11 (Rev. Ver.); 1 John iv. 17). The only Scripture cited for this doctrine of death sanctification is Rom. vi. 7: "He that is dead is free from sin." This evidently means (see verse 6), he who has died unto sin is freed or justified (Rev. Ver.) from sin. This text, found by the "Brethren," escaped the keen eyes of the whole Westminster Assembly, who could find nothing in proof of this point better than Heb. xii, 23: "the spirits of just men made perfect," assuming the point in proof that they were made perfect in death. The Greek scholar will note that the text reads, not "perfected spirits," but the "spirits of perfected just (men)," implying perfection in this life. Yet the old man is to be quite vigorously choked down and kept under till death comes to the rescue and brings that good riddance which the Father, Son, and Holy Spirit, could not bestow. He is to be reckoned as dead by a kind of pious fiction, though he is as lusty and vigorous as ever. That Scripture which says "that the body of sin might be destroyed" is explained to signify, "be repressed" and "rendered inactive"; and those Scriptures in which the old man, or the flesh, is to be crucified, mortified, or killed, are all understood to imply a life-long torture on the cross — a killing that continues through scores of years. Says J. Denham Smith, a conspicuous Plymouth theologian, in a standard theological tract: "The two natures remain in him unchanged. His old nature is not modified or ameliorated by the impartation of the new; nor, on the other hand, does the new nature become soiled or corrupted by reason of its co-existence in the same being with the old.

They remain the same. There is no blending or amalgamation. They are essentially and eternally distinct. The old nature is unalterably and incurably corrupt, while the new nature is divinely pure in its essence."

This doctrine of the two natures is not completely stated till the fact is brought out that neither is regarded as responsible for the acts of the other. For they are conceived of as persons. If the flesh of the believer behaves badly, that is none of the believer's business. He does not live in that department of his being, and hence has no responsibility for its evil deeds. The "flesh was condemned on the cross and is under sentence," why should I worry about it? This reminds us of the story of the English bishop and his servant, who reproved him for profanity. The bishop, who was a member of the house of lords, replied, that he swore as a lord, not as a bishop. "But," queried the servant, "when the devil gets the lord, what will become of the bishop?"

The favorite method of exegesis of 1 John iii. 9, is to substitute "whatsoever" for "whosoever," and to say, "that part of our nature that is born of God does not commit sin," the unregenerate part will continue to sin. This is the style of exegesis: "We have a right to read the text thus: '*Whatsoever* is born of God doth not sin.' We are double creatures all the way through. That part of us that is born of God does not sin. Sin is decreasing; righteousness is growing. So we need not feel discouraged if we find ourselves going astray, if the purpose of our heart is toward God. We are confident of constant progression — sure of being better in the other life than here. It is always first the blade, then the ear, after that the full corn in the ear. The Apostle tells us that religion brings us great assurance. We know we shall be like Him — how little like Him now! We are a long way from the perfect pattern of Christ, of being like Him in character, with not a stain upon the soul's whiteness. Feed your soul on the thought of better things to come. Look for the hour when He shall appear and we shall be like Him."

At this point the following questions are pertinent: —

1. Have we any right to lower the standard of character required in the Scriptures to suit the state of "those who are called Christians"? Is not such an expounder guilty of a perversion of the Holy Scriptures?

2. How high a rank is that theology entitled to which discrowns man in order to save him; which changes him from a "who" to a "what," from a person to a thing, in order to keep him from sinning? Does such a theology emphasize the sacredness and dignity of man? Does it honor the Holy Spirit to teach that He begets impersonal "whatsoevers," instead of personal "whomsoevers"?

3. In the light of this exposition, what becomes of St. John's sharply defined line sepa-

rating "the children of God" and "the children of the devil"? For in the very next verse to the text he says: "In this" — the fact of not sinning — "the children of God are manifest, and the children of the devil" — in the fact of their sinning. This exposition not only "tears down the fence between the Lord's garden and the devil's common," but it actually binds up the child of God and the child of the devil in a single personality, impossible to be classified either with the righteous or the wicked.

4. Is the human being of such a double nature that a part of him may be holy, and a part commit sin?

5. Is not the action of the free will an element of every moral act, and can the will at one and the same time sin and abstain from sin?

6. If such a moral philosophy is good in the pulpit, would it not be good at the bar? Could not the lawyer plead that the part of the

accused which is born of God is innocent of the crime, and that it is only the unregenerate part that has done the mischief, and therefore the regenerate part should be acquitted?

Would not any judge, endowed with average common sense, sentence the unregenerate part to the gallows, and tell the regenerate part to look out for itself? The soul that sinneth — the undivided soul — it shall die.

7. Is there any analogy in the natural world for a partial birth — a part being born at one time and a part forty or fifty years afterward? A hearer of this exposition very properly asks me the question: "What if a person should die before he gets wholly born?"

8. Is the expounder right in his interpretation of assurance, that it does not relate to present knowledge of forgiveness and of entire sanctification, but to the final perseverance of the saints? Does it not always relate to a knowledge of our present acceptance with God, except this one expression, "the assurance of hope"?

9. Is freedom from sin ever presented as an object of hope in the future? Is entire sanctification ever classified with the good things to come, such as the second coming of Christ, the resurrection and glorification of the body, and the rewards of Heaven?

10. Does not St. John, in this very epistle, declare, that as Jesus is, so are Christians in this world? Does the likeness of Christ which believers shall have when they shall see Him, consist in the fact of their being then sanctified, or rather in the fact of both soul and body then glorified?

11. Our last question is this: Is Antinomianism getting up out of its grave in New England? For the innermost essence of this error is, that it destroys human responsibility for sin, by saddling it all upon the flesh, " the old man," who turns out at last a mere mythical person who cannot be found in the Day of Judgment.

We are impressed, in reading the Plymouth writings, with the perpetual confusion of the term, "sinful flesh," with the body, as though sin could be predicated of the material part of man. Some even speak of the hand and the foot as committing sin. Thus the old error of Oriental philosophy and of Gnosticism, that inherent and unconquerable evil lurks in matter, lies at the bottom of the Plymouth theology.

Of course they strenuously antagonize inwrought and personal holiness as an utter impossibility, since the old man has a lease of the soul which does not expire till death. Yet they insist that they are perfectly holy in Christ "up there," while perfectly carnal and corrupt "down here" in their moral state. They dwell *ad nauseam* upon the distinction between the *standing* in Christ and the *state*. The standing in Christ attained by a single act of faith is the great and decisive thing; the moral state is a small affair, having not the least power to damage the standing. David in Uriah's bed, and with hands red with his blood, was in a sad moral predicament indeed, so far as his moral state was concerned, but his judicial standing in Christ was not in the least impaired. All that he lost was his communion with God; all that he sought for was restored *joy* — "Restore Thou unto me the joy of Thy salvation." God did not see his adultery and murder. These were covered with the blood of atonement shed in the Divine purpose before the foundation of the world, and put away forever before David was born. A favorite proof text for this abominable dogma, which lays the axe at the root of the whole system of Christian morals, is Num. xxiii. 21: "He hath not beheld iniquity in Jacob, neither hath he seen perverseness in Israel," correctly rendered by Rosenmüller: "God cannot endure to behold iniquity cast upon Jacob, nor can He bear to see affliction, vexation, trouble, wrought against Israel." Some such must be the meaning of this text. The Plymouth exegesis makes it positively deny the omniscence of God, and flatly contradict His declaration: "Because all these men which have seen My glory, and My miracles which I did in Egypt and in the wilderness, have tempted Me now these ten times, and have not hearkened to My voice; surely they shall not see the land which I swear unto their fathers, neither shall any of them that provoked me see it" (Num. xiv. 22, 23). God not only saw the sins of Israel, but He kept accurate account of their number, and so indignant was He that He purposed to smite and disinherit the whole nation, and raise up a better one from Moses (Num. xiv. 12).

The doctrine that the believer is seen only in Christ, and is regarded as pure as Christ Himself, is founded on his incorporation into the glorified human and Divine Person in heaven. The first act of faith is the occasion on which the Holy Spirit eternally incorporates the believer into the risen and glorified body of Jesus Christ. "Since," as Mr. Darby said to the writer, "Jesus does not walk about in heaven dropping off fingers and toes," it follows that every believer once incorporated into Christ is absolutely sure of ultimate salvation. The certainty is forever beyond contingencies. No act of sin, even murder, can remove us from our standing in Christ. Sin may obstruct communion, and leave the soul in sadness and darkness for a season; but since, as Shakspeare says, "All is well that ends well," sin in a believer is well since it ends in eternal life. For a proof of this doctrine, Eph. v. 30 is quoted: "For we are members of His body." The clause, "of His flesh and of His bones," which is rejected by the Revised Version as spurious, is strongly emphasized as a proof of a literal incorporation into the person of Christ. A little attention to the context will show that literal embodiment in Christ cannot be meant without implying the actual incorporation of the husband and wife in "one flesh." If it be said, this is just what marriage produces, we reply, that the "one flesh" of wedlock becomes two through infidelity to the marriage vow (Matt.

v. 32). Sin destroys the soul's marriage with Christ, and brings about a divorce which may become eternal (James iv. 4–6, Rev. Ver). Another favorite proof-text is Eph. ii. 6, which is understood as teaching that all believers are, in their judicial standing, literally "sitting together in heavenly places in Christ Jesus." Another proof-text is found in the oft-recurring words, "in Christ."

It may be safely said that the Plymouth doctrines find their basis in a literalizing of figures, ingenious allegorizing of facts, and a straining of types. The best specimens of typology run wild, are found in the Plymouth commentaries. For instance: In order to prove that it was not the mission of the Comforter to sanctify the pentecostal Church, and to destroy sin in the hearts of full believers, this is the line of argument which is thought to be unanswerable: Leaven always stands for sin. In Lev. xxiii. 16, 17, is the command to put leaven into the bread for Pentecost. Therefore there was sin in the Pentecostal Church after it was filled with the Holy Spirit, whose office is not to cleanse believers from all sin, but to incorporate them into Christ up in the sky. This is the argument of their greatest annotator, M'Intosh, whose exegetical skill and spiritual insight are by some of "the Brethren" attributed to an inspiration almost plenary. Says another writer, J. R. C.: "We know that Moses in the law spake of Christ. These ancient enactments were shadows, in many, if not in all, cases, of good things to come." Then from the Mosaic requirement that "the man who hath taken a wife shall not go out to war, but shall be free at home one year to cheer his wife," he gravely argues that this signifies that Christ will not go forth to battle until He has remained with the saints a certain period at home in a kind of honeymoon. Here is a specimen of Major Whittle's typology, whose doctrines are all drawn from the Plymouth Brethren: First, he assumes, without a particle of proof, that the ark is a type of Christ. Secondly, all who went into the ark in the old world came out in the new; none died, none were lost. Hence all who are once in Christ will be infallibly saved! Admit the premises, and the demonstration is irresistible.

These are only a few specimens of the logic of types when handled by an ingenious man, eager to find biblical proofs for un-Scriptural doctrines. The great master of this fallacious treatment of God's Word, the wizzard who can give a Scriptural flavor to tenets most repugnant to the sacred oracles, is Andrew Jukes. Whether one of the "Brethren," I know not; but he is unexcelled in their typological sleight of hand, even going beyond his teachers and demonstrating the ultimate restoration of all the wicked in hell to holiness and heaven. Evangelical minds should be on their guard against this subtle method of instilling dangerous theological errors. There is a large class of minds which are easily captivated by types which are purely fanciful, the cunning inventions of men.

CHAPTER IV.

THE PLYMOUTH BRETHREN — (*Continued*).

A CARDINAL Plymouth tenet is the necessary continuance of the flesh, or the old man, and his abiding, unchanged, with the new man, till death. Regeneration has no effect on the old man by way of improvement or extinction. He is incapable of becoming better, and has a life-lease in the believer's soul. The personality, or what says *I*, may put itself under the leadership of either the new nature or the old for an indefinite period without detriment to the standing, only the communion is obstructed when the old Adam is at the helm. The best illustration of the Christian soul is, that it is a tenement with two rooms. The spiritual apartment faces the sun, and the fleshly room is in the rear, turned from the sun. The believer, once sure of his standing in Christ, may live in the front room and bask in the sunshine, or he may retire into the back room and live in the shade. He is exhorted to live in the front room, and to keep the back room locked, if he would have unbroken happiness through cloudless communion with God. But if he should disregard the exhortation, and, owl-like, should dwell amid the darkness all his days, he is just as sure at last of the inheritance of the saints in light, though he was not partial to the light while dwelling in his double tenement on the earth.

These teachers have a special hostility to the Weslyan doctrine of Christian perfection, against which they oppose perfection in Christ. They are very shy of the term "perfect love," since this, as used by St. John, evidently refers to our love to God: "Herein is our love made perfect." This is not God's love to us, as some say, "for," says Alford, "this is forbidden by the whole context." Inwrought personal holiness is denied, as ministering to pride, while a constant declaration of inward vileness, and of a fictitious purity, by the imputation of Christ's purity, is supposed to conduce to our humility and Christ's exaltation.

The Plymouth idea of entire sanctification is exceedingly complex and contradictory. First, in our standing we are as holy as Christ; secondly, in our flesh we are perfectly vile, the old man being incapable of improvement; thirdly, the new man is perfectly pure, being a new creature by the Spirit, and hence not needing sanctification. This statement is highly suggestive of the celebrated kettle plea:—

1. Our client never borrowed the kettle; 2. It was cracked when he borrowed it; 3. It was whole when he returned it.

But, nevertheless, there is an exhortation to practical holiness in most of the writings of the Brethren, on this wise: "Be holy down here because ye are holy up there" (in Christ). "Strive to make your state correspond with your standing." Yet this motive to Christian purity is neutralized by the assurance that the believer's standing in Christ is eternal anyhow, just as the exhortation to sinners to repentance by a Universalist is a motive of no force, since ultimate salvation is certain. Says M'Intosh: "God will never reverse His decision as to what His people are as to standing." "Israel's blessedness and security are made to depend, not on *themselves*, but on the faithfulness of Jehovah." "We must never measure the standing by the state, but always the state by the standing. To lower the standing because of the state, is to give the death-blow to all progress in practical Christianity." That is to say, the fruit must always be judged by the tree; to judge the tree by the fruit, is to give the death-blow to practical pomology.

The opening verse of 2 Cor. xii., speaks of visions and revelations of the Lord; the closing verse condemns uncleanness and fornication and lasciviousness not repented of. "In the former," says M'Intosh, "we have the *positive standing* of the Christian; in the latter, the *possible state* into which he may fall if not watchful." Yet he keeps his Christly standing amid all his swinish wallowings! This is Plymouth Brethrenism in a nut-shell. Here is another: "In John xiii. the Lord Jesus looks at His disciples and pronounces them 'clean every whit'; although in a few hours one of them was to curse and swear that he did not know Him. So vast is the difference between what we are in ourselves and what we are in Christ — between our positive standing and our possible state." (Notes on Leviticus.)

These theologians make a nice distinction between *conscience* of sin and *consciousness* of sins, where neither the Bible nor moral science affords the least ground for this distinction. "The former," say they, "is guilt; the latter is the normal experience of all believers. They ever feel the motions of sin within their hearts." Whereas conscience is nothing more than consciousness when the question of right or wrong is before the mind.

Here is another distinction vital to the Plymouth system: "It is of the utmost importance that we accurately distinguish between sin *in the flesh* and sin *on the conscience*. If we confound these two, our souls must, necessarily, be unhinged, and our worship marred." Then follows the Scriptural distinction in 1 John i. 8–10: "'If we say that we have *no* sin (*in us*), we deceive ourselves, and the truth is not in us.' In the next verse we find the sin *on* us— 'the blood of Jesus Christ cleanseth us from *all* sin.'" What becomes of the sin *in* us when *all* sin is cleansed, the writer does not deign to say; but he does say that, "Here the distinction between sin *in* us and sin *on*, is fully brought out and established."

It is so "fully brought out" that it took 1,800 years for Bible readers to discover it, and then only through Plymouth eye-glasses! From Augustine to Darby this has been a standing proof-text against entire sanctification, which is as plainly taught in the passage as the sun in the heavens. Let any candid mind read the context, and he will see that the clause, "If we say we have no sin," means, if any unregenerate man denies that he has any sin which needs the atonement, or that he has ever sinned, as it is in verse ten, he deceives himself. No writer would so stultify himself as to say that he who is cleansed from all sin in the seventh verse, is a dupe and a liar in the eighth verse, if he testifies to the all-cleansing blood. John must be written down as utterly self-contradictory to say that he that is born of God sinneth not, and then brand with deception and falsehood the man who should profess that by grace he was kept from sin. Yet this passage, wrenched from its context, is the proof constantly reiterated, that there is no salvation from sin in this life. The absurdity of this text as a proof of indwelling sin, as the highest attainable state of the Christian, and of self-deception on the part of the person who professes entire inward cleansing, is akin to that of advertising a complete cure of cancers, and then branding as false every testimony to such a cure.

Another text constantly urged by them, in utter disregard of the context, is Gal. v. 17, which, by that fallacy in logic called "begging the question," they assume to be descriptive of the most perfect specimen of the Spirit's work in a human soul, whereas St. Paul is writing to a backsliding church. "I marvel," says he, as translated by Dean Alford, "that ye are so soon removing from Him that called you in the grace of Christ, unto a different Gospel." Again: "Are ye so foolish? Having begun in the Spirit, are ye now being made perfect in the flesh?"

In believers, in this mixed moral state, a struggle is going on between the flesh and the spirit. The fallacy lies in the assumption, that the best Christians are in this state, against the positive testimony of St. Paul: "I have been crucified with Christ; and it is no longer I that live, but Christ that liveth in me."

The doctrine of assurance is strongly emphasized by these Christians as the privilege of all who are in Christ. They are very earnest in their condemnation of the "hope-so" experience, and they insist on a clear and undoubted knowledge of the forgiveness of sins and adoption into the family of God. But this truth, when joined with the pernicious doctrine of eternal incorporation into the glorified body of Christ, removes the safeguard against sin, which old-fashioned Calvinism set up, in the uncertainty which every Christian was taught that he must feel respecting his acceptance with God.

Both Calvinism and Arminianism have checks which deter believers from sin. The Arminian is told that the holiest saint on earth may fall from grace and drop into hell. The Calvinist is restrained from abusing the doctrine of unconditional election by the consideration, that no man may, beyond a doubt, know that his own name is on the secret register of God's chosen ones. This ignorance inspires a healthful solicitude promotive of watchfulness and persevering fidelity in the Calvinist, just as the possibility of total and final apostasy tends to conserve the purity of the Arminian. The Plymouth Brethren drop both of these safeguards by uniting, with eternal incorporation into Christ, a present and absolute assurance of that fact. There may be a few souls who would not be put in imminent peril by the revelation, that their eternal salvation is secured beyond a peradventure; but the mass of believers would become dizzy, if suddenly lifted to such a height, and many would fall into sin. Human nature at its best estate can never be safely released from the salutary restraint of fear. Hence we predict that great moral disasters will follow the general prevalence of the teachings of Mr. Darby and his school.

In this matter of assurance, how much more guarded are the utterances of John Wesley, who teaches the certain knowledge of justification by faith, with appropriate safeguards.

"Let none ever presume to rest in any supposed testimony of the Spirit which is separate from the fruit of it." This, translated into the Plymouth idiom, would read thus: "Let none ever presume to rest in any supposed *standing* in Christ while his actual *state* of character is not radiant with all the excellences of Christ." "Let no one who is in a state of wilful sin, imagine that he has a standing in Christ pure and clear before the throne of God, for his standing in heaven is the same as his state on earth."

In perfect accord with this absolute assurance of final salvation, is the denial of the general judgment as taught in all orthodox creeds. If the saints have a through ticket for heaven, why should they stand before the judgment seat of Christ? The favorite proof-text, ever on the lips of the Brethren, is John v. 24, with the comment that "condemnation" should be translated "judgment." To show how far this fails to prove the doctrine for which it is quoted, I will adduce Alford's note Anglicizing the Greek: "The believing and the having eternal life are commensurate; where the faith is, the possession of eternal life is; and when the one remits, the other is forfeited. But here the faith is set before us as an *enduring* faith, and its effects are described in their completion (See Eph. i. 19, 20)." "He who believeth" (perseveringly) "comes not into, has no concern with, the separation (*krisis*), the damnatory part of the judgment." All the texts which teach the simultaneous judgment of all the human family are ingeniously explained away by partial judgments strung along through the future, after the doctrine of Swedenborg, in order to make way for this new doctrine, that the saints will not be before Christ's judgment tribunal in the last day. We shall show the fallacy of these explanations when we come to the discussion of the Plymouth scheme of eschatology, or last things.

THE SINS OF BELIEVERS ARE NOT REAL SINS.

This is a necessary inference from the assured exemption of believers from condemnation, however deep their fall into gross sins. For this exemption implies the absence of guilt. Those acts which entail no guilt cannot be real sins. If they appear to be sins, their appearance is deceptive. Hence, a distinguished English doctor of divinity could say in the pulpit, "A believer may be assured of pardon as soon as he commits any sin, even adultery and murder. Sins are but scarecrows and bugbears, to frighten ignorant children, but men of understanding see they are counterfeit things."

The author has heard Dr. Brooks, of St. Louis, assert that the sins of believers materially differ from the sins of unbelievers, hinting that they are not real sins in God's eyes, because He sees the believer and all his acts only in Jesus Christ. This is the logical conclusion from the premises that character is transferable, that Jesus Christ on the cross became a sinner, and was punished, while we, by a single act of faith, assume His righteousness by an inalienable incorporation into His glorified person in heaven, and are ever afterward viewed by God as possessing all His moral excellencies, among which is sinlessness.

What an opiate to the accusing conscience! what a weakening of the divine safeguards against sin, set up in man's moral constitution, are manifest on the very face of such a theological tenet! The chief barrier against sin is removed, and sinning is made easy. With ordinary human beings, even after regeneration, facility for sinning with impunity becomes a tremendous temptation, and to most men an irresistible incentive to sin. If God has solemnly pronounced "woe to them that call (moral) evil good, and (moral) good evil," what must be His sentence against those who entirely rub out the broad boundary line between them by teaching that the willful violation of the known law of God is only a seeming, but not a real sin? Yet this is the inevitable outcome of the doctrine that there never can be condemnation to them who are in Christ. The case is aggravated by the denial of the possibility of entire sanctification in this life, and by the assertion that the flesh, the sinward bent of the soul, must remain until it is eradicated by physical death. Broadcast these twin doctrines throughout christendom, that believers are incapable of real sin, and that the sin principle is a necessity in every human heart during this life, defying the blood of Christ to purge it away, and the Christian Church will need myriads of patient toilers to grub up these seeds of immoralities, more baneful than the Canada thistle is to the farmers of this western world.

This whole question of the believer's relation to God's law has been discussed by the theological giants of past generations. I quote from Baxter's Aphorisms on Justification, an epitome made by J. Wesley: "As there are two covenants, with their distinct conditions, so there is a twofold righteousness, and both of them absolutely necessary for salvation. Our righteousness of the first covenant (under the remediless, Christless, Adamic law) is not personal, or consisteth not in any actions preferred by us; for we never personally satisfied the law (of innocence), but it is wholly without us, in Christ. In this sense every Christian disclaimeth his own righteousness, or his own works. Those only shall be in Christ legally righteous who believe and OBEY the Gospel, and so are in themselves evangelically righteous. Though Christ performed the conditions of the law (of Paradisaical innocence), and made satisfaction for our non-performance, YET WE OURSELVES MUST PERFORM THE CONDITIONS OF THE GOSPEL. These (last) two propositions seem to me so clear, that I wonder that any able divines should deny them. Methinks they should be articles of our creed, and a part of children's catechisms. To affirm that our evangelical or new-covenant righteousness is in Christ, and not in ourselves, or performed by Christ, and not by ourselves, is such a monstrous piece of Antinomian doctrine as no man, who knows the nature and difference of the covenants, can possibly entertain." (Bax. Aphor. Prop. 14–17.) Thus speaks this pious, practical, well-balanced dissenter against the fatal errors arising from confounding the Adamic law with the law of Christ, the first demanding of a perfect man a faultless life, the other requiring an imperfect man, inheriting damaged intellectual and moral powers, to render perfect, that is, pure love, to God his Heavenly Father, through Christ his adorable Saviour, with the assistance of regenerating and sanctifying grace.

It was the clearly discerned distinction between the two covenants which prompted good Bishop Hopkins to make this paradoxical resolution: "So to BELIEVE, so to rest on the merits of Christ, as if I had never wrought anything; and withal so to WORK, as if I were only to be saved by my own merits." To give each of these its due in practice, is the very height and depth of Christian perfection.

MODERN ANTINOMIANISM EXAMINED.

The new Antinomianism does not make Calvinism prominent by any formal statement. It is rather implied than expressed. Nothing is said of sovereign decrees and of unconditional election. For this reason it does not specially offend Arminians, while its doctrine of the final perseverance of all believers is a tenet very pleasing to those who hold Calvinism, with its modern alleviations, the only form still extant in New England. For these reasons this great error is well adapted to become widespread in both these great branches of orthodoxy.

There is a class of people who are specially pleased to see the Gospel set in antagonism with the law, and they breathe more easily when they are assured that God's law, as the rule of life, is abrogated by the Gospel. This repugnance of the Gospel to the moral law is one of the primal errors of all Antinomians. But the form which this antagonism takes, is peculiar to the modern Antinomianism. This is the difference between the believer's standing in Christ, and his actual moral state. These bear no relation to each other. The state may be utterly bad, while the standing be perfectly good. Like the first brick in a row, Jesus only is seen by the eye of God, the defects of the others, covered by Him, are not seen; the perfections of Jesus being seen instead. This standing, attained by the first act of faith, is inalienable and everlasting.

The influence of this doctrine of an eternal and inalienable standing in Christ, and of exemption from the day of judgment, must, in many cases, be disastrous. The removal of the wholesome safeguard found in the fear of being morally shipwrecked and cast away, must tend to looseness of living in not a few cases. It is possible that a few might suffer no detriment from embracing such a theory, but they would be exceptions. Most people live below, not above their creed. How can a man, amid the fierce temptations of life, sing the following verses, and be just as watchful against sin as before? Especially, how can one in whom the old man exists in full strength?

> "Rejoice, rejoice, my soul,
>   Rejoice in sin forgiven;
> The blood of Christ hath made thee whole;
>   For thee His life was given.
>
> "Rejoice in peace made sure:
>   *No judgment now for thee;*
> Thy conscience purged, thy life secure,
>   *More safe thou canst not be.*"

Heaven itself can afford no greater safety! Is there no moral peril in preaching such a doctrine to men in the furnace of temptation? In all my study of human nature, I have found that the removal of barriers against sin is a tremendous incentive to its commission.

Repentance Slighted.

At another point, the Plymouth system is open to criticism — its neglect of, or very slight emphasis on, the need of repentance. This is in keeping with its Antinomian tendencies. I quote from Dr. Robert Anderson's book, — "The Gospel and its Ministry," — a book highly commended by Mr. Moody, to verify this criticism, and to show that this defect is not an oversight, but a part of the system, the justification of which is attempted in this quotation: "The soundest and fullest Gospel preaching need not include any mention of the word (repentance). Neither as verb or noun does it occur in the Epistle to the Romans, — God's great doctrinal treatise on redemption and righteousness, — save in the warnings of the second chapter. And the Gospel-book of all the Bible will be searched in vain for a single mention of it. The beloved Disciple wrote His Gospel, that men might believe and live, and His Epistle followed, to confirm believers in the simplicity and certainty of their faith; but yet, from end to end of them, the word 'repent' or 'repentance' never once occurs." This proves nothing. It is manifest to every student, that the synoptic Gospels, which are full of repentance, present a different phase of Christ's teaching from John's Gospel. Again, it would not be natural to look for exhortations to repentance in epistles to believers, whether John's epistles or Paul's. To find these, let us turn to the reports of the Apostle's sermons to the unconverted, in the Acts, and we will find repentance preached in due proportion to other duties. See the concordance, in which these words will be found in the Acts eleven times. It must be carefully remembered that, though the word "believe" occurs about a hundred times in John's Gospel, and "repent" is not found even once, John's "believe" is so large in its meaning that it comprehends conversion, or turning from sin, as well as trusting in Christ. This fulness of meaning must not be neglected, but must be magnified by him who would get John's deep meaning. He can never be quoted to support Antinomianism. The preaching of repentance in no way belittles faith in Jesus, the sole condition of forgiveness, but it is the indispensable prerequisite to its exercise. Hence, repentance must be earnestly preached.

CHAPTER V.

ANTINOMIAN FAITH.

WE look in vain in all these writers of the Antinomian school, whether ancient or modern, for any adequate definitions of saving faith. After a faithful and patient study, extending through ten years, I can find in these writings no better notion of faith than a bare * intellectual assent to the fact that Jesus put away sin once and forever on His cross. There is no preliminary to this mental act, such as a heart-felt conviction of sin, and eternal abandonment of it in purpose and in reality. Nor is there any test of this faith in the genuineness of its fruits. The evangelical definition of saving faith is utterly ignored,— that it has its root in genuine repentance, its bud and blossom in joyful obedience, and its fruitage in holiness of heart and life; that in addition to the assent of

* See Sandeman's epitaph in App.

the intellect, — the fruitless faith of devils (James ii. 19), — there must be the consent of the will, the Christward movement of the moral sensibilities, and an unwavering reliance on Him, and on Him alone, as a present Saviour. Nor do the Antinomians teach that faith is continuous — a life-long outgoing of the heart in glad obedience — but rather that its efficacy is concentrated into a single act of assent to a past fact, an act which forever and forever justifies. We can easily predict the character of the edifice built upon a foundation so defective. On such a corner-stone we do not expect to find a love which purifies the heart and overcomes the world, a hunger and thirst after righteousness, an eager pursuit of holiness, and "pressing on unto perfection" (Heb. vi. 1, Rev. Ver.), and that "perfect love which casteth out all fear that has torment." We find rather a dry, intellectual religion, tenacious of its speculative theory, indifferent to inward and outward holiness, and reveling in imaginary graces, or, rather, in the perfections of Christ falsely imputed to themselves, and preferring to keep the old man alive rather than his summary crucifixion, in order "that the body of sin may be destroyed." We find a system which is a great comfort to the backslider in heart and life, and a pleasant refuge to those who have lost their inheritance among the sanctified, into which they once entered when under better religious instruction.

We have thus far spoken of an indefinite Antinomian faith; we now proceed to speak of

FAITH VERSUS FEELING.

"The power of God," says Fletcher, "is frequently talked of, but rarely felt, and too often cried down under the despicable name of *frames* and *feelings*."

"If I had a mind," said the eloquent George Whitefield, "to hinder the progress of the Gospel, and to establish the kingdom of darkness, I would go about telling people they might have the Spirit of God, and yet not feel it," or which is much the same, that the pardon which

Christ procured *for* them is already obtained *by* them, whether they enjoy the sense of it or not.

This is the kind of faith which multitudes of souls in utter spiritual barrenness are resting in for eternal life. They are exhorted to beware of looking for any changed feeling, that feeling is inconsistent with true faith. Says John Wesley, "It is easy to satisfy ourselves without being possessed of the holiness and happiness of the Gospel. It is easy to call these (holiness and happiness) frames and feelings, and then to oppose faith to one and Christ to the other. Frames (allowing the expression) are no other than heavenly tempers, the mind that was in Christ; feelings are the Divine consolations of the Holy Ghost shed abroad in the heart of him that truly believes. And wherever faith is, and wherever Christ is, there are these blessed frames and feelings. If they are not in us, it is a sure sign that though the wilderness become a pool, the pool is become a wilderness again." (*Note on Peter* iii. 18).

This is the process of inculcating this kind

of faith. The religious teacher sits down in the inquiry room, by the side of the seeker, opens his Bible at Romans x. 9, and reads: "If thou shalt confess with thy mouth the Lord Jesus (Jesus *as* Lord, Rev. Ver.), and shalt believe in thy heart that God hath raised him from the dead, thou shalt be saved." Do you confess that Jesus is your Lord? Yes. Do you believe that He arose from the dead? Yes. Well, praise the Lord, you are born again! you have found eternal life. But I do not experience any inward change. Never mind that; you are to believe without any feeling. If you look for feeling as the ground of your faith that you are now a child of God, you dishonor the Word. The Word says that you are saved, and you ought to believe the Bible. It is weak and childish to be looking for any change in your feelings. I strongly advise you to be baptized and join the Church. You have fulfilled the conditions of salvation. You are henceforth to count yourself a Christian, and by a resolved will to crush out all doubts respecting your conversion, whenever they arise. For they will arise. All true Christians have doubts of this kind. It is an evidence that they have a good hope in Christ. But, dear pastor, is this all there is in the new birth? I expected I should have unspeakable joy, arising from a sense of burning love. I thought I should be sure that I was saved by some inward impression by the Holy Ghost. Oh, says the pastor, you are not to expect a miraculous conversion. That kind is limited to the Apostolic age.

Sin "in," and Sin "on," the Soul.*

Through all their books and innumerable tracts runs a distinction between the prepositions "in" and "on." It is the aim of the Gospel to deliver from sin "on" the soul, but not from sin "in" the heart, till we pass through the gate of death. In other words, justification is affirmed, but entire sanctification in the present life is denied. The blood of Jesus Christ is efficacious for the removal of

* See words of Dr. Brooks in App.

actual sins, but it fails to eradicate the sin principle, or inbred sin, till physical death comes to the aid of atonement, and completes its saving power. Thus the penalty of sin becomes its destroyer. "Death, that foul monster, the offspring of sin, shall have the important honor of killing his father," says Fletcher. "He alone is to give the great, the last, the decisive blow." In vain do we call for Scripture proofs for death sanctification, and for the important distinction between "in" and "on." When those Scriptures are cited which teach immediate perfect cleansing from all sin, as in 1 John i. 7, 9, we are assured that the verb "cleanse" here means judicial clearance, or justification, and not inherent purification. But this involves St. John in the Romish doctrine of good works as a condition of justification — "If we walk in the light." This is certainly a course of good works prescribed as a condition of cleansing. If this is pardon, we have a condition unknown to St. Paul. But we have as great a difficulty in passages which urge us to cleanse ourselves, as 2 Cor. vii. 1. Here we have a cluster of absurdities. (1.) Self-justification: "Let us cleanse ourselves." (2.) Justification is divided and distributed into two parts, "flesh and spirit"— a piece-meal pardon! (3.) "Filthiness" is a state. How can a state be justified, or have judicial clearance or acquittal?

It is easy to see that sin "in" the believer, who has been adopted into the family of God (2 Cor. vi. 18), or inbred, original depravity, is here intended, and the Corinthians are exhorted to seek its entire purgation as a condition to "perfecting holiness in the fear of the Lord."

Not Under the Law.

"Free from the law, oh, happy condition!"

This is a verse which should never be sung except with those safeguards which the author of the hymn has not been careful to set up.

(1.) It is true that all mankind are, by the

atonement, forever freed from the necessity of pleading that we have perfectly kept the law, in order to acceptance with God. We are freed from the necessity of legal justification. Such a necessity would shut up a sinful race in eternal despair. We are freed from the law *as the ground of justification.* Our ground of justification is the blood of Christ shed for us.

(2.) Nor are true believers, who have received the Spirit of adoption, under the law *as the impulse to service.* They are not spurred on to activity by the threatened penalties of God's law. Love to the Law-giver has taken the place of fear of the law as a motive. This is specially true of those advanced believers, out of whom perfect love has cast all servile, tormenting fear. Before emerging into this experience, there is a blending of fear and love as motives to service. In this state the believer is not wholly delivered from legalism. But the law is put into the heart of the full believer, and its fulfillment is spontaneous and free. "I will run the way of Thy commandments when Thou shalt enlarge my heart." The Septuagint Version, used by our Lord Jesus, reads: "I have run. . . . Since," etc. "Without the law," says St. Paul, as an outward yoke laid upon the neck, "but under law to Christ." Love to Christ absorbs into itself all the principles of the moral law, and prompts to their glad performance. Hence, "Love is the fulfillment of the law." This is the meaning of Rom. vii. 6, as translated in the Revision which corrects the blunder of King James' version from a faulty MS., making the law of God die, instead of the believer's dying to it; that is, ceasing to be actuated by its terrors, and becoming obedient from the new principle of love. "But now we have been discharged from the law, having died to that wherein we were holden; so that WE SERVE IN NEWNESS OF THE SPIRIT, and not in the oldness of the letter."

(3.) We are free from the law *as the instrument of our sanctification*. Christ has become our sanctification by purchasing with His blood the gift of the Holy Spirit. He is called "holy," not as a peculiar attribute, distinguishing Him from the Father and the Son, but because it is His great office to make men holy. We are "elect through sanctification of the Spirit and belief of the truth."

(4.) Christ has freed us from the *ceremonial law*.

(5.) Believers in Christ are not delivered from the moral law, *as the rule of life*. The form of this law may change, but the essence is as immutable as its Author, out of whose bosom it goes forth. If believers were free from the law, as a rule of life, we should be obliged to change the verse —

"Free from the law, oh, wretched condition"!

A moral intelligence, whether man or angel, thus freed from his proper norm, would dash into ruins like a locomotive of an express train freed from the rails. As the rails give direction to the mighty momentum of the train, so is the law designed to direct our moral progress to a destiny of unspeakable blessedness. Disobedience derails and destroys. Hence the law is a blessing of unspeakable value. The soul that despises it is in imminent peril. The theology which teaches that men mount to a "happy condition," by ridding themselves of the beneficent guidance of the moral law, merits the condemnation of all Christians. Jesus is a Law-giver to control, as well as a Redeemer to save.

The Sinner has Nothing to Do.

> "Nothing, either great or small,
> Nothing, sinner, no;
> Jesus died and paid it all,
> Long, long ago."

All that Jesus has done for the sinner will do him no good till he personally appropriates, by a faith which requires the highest effort to exercise, and which prompts to a continued course of good works. "This is the work of

God — which He requires — that ye believe in His Son." In all cases there must be repentance and its fruits, forsaking wicked ways, and turning to God. In the case of the unbelieving Jews there were two severe preliminary works before they could believe. They must conquer their love for human honor, and through the use of prevenient grace, rise to the position where they are swayed by the honor that comes from God only, or the only God. *Hic labor, hoc opus est* — this is work, this is toil. Jesus sets another task before the Jews before they can believe in Him. They must believe in Moses. Men cannot indolently neglect inferior light, and, at a single bound, spring up to the highest exercise of faith in Jesus, the Light of the world. They must be of the truth before they can come to Him who is the Truth. They must so love the truth already within their reach as to be willing to search for it diligently, and to follow wherever the truth leads. This implies self-denial and cross-bearing, even before Jesus is apprehended as their Saviour. Then having found Him, they must consecrate all their powers of service to do His will; they must work while the day lasts. These works are rewardable, though not meritorious, in the sense of putting God under obligation to compensate the doers. In the light of these truths the following verses have an Antinomian sound: —

> "Cast your deadly 'doing' down —
> Down at Jesus' feet;
> Stand in Him, in Him alone,
> Gloriously complete.
>
> "Cease your doing; all was done
> Long, long ago.
>
> "'Doing' is a deadly thing —
> 'Doing' ends in death."

There is a call in this latter quarter of the nineteenth century for St. James to go through the world preaching from his favorite text: "Faith without works is dead." Sinners are not saved by works, but they must work to be saved. "Work out your salvation with fear and trembling. Ye are workers together with God."

THE FLESH REMAINS FLESH.

Two natures co-existing in the believer in his best possible earthly state, is proved by John iii. 6, which is amended to read thus: "That which is born of the flesh is flesh, *and remains flesh*, and that which is born of the Spirit is spirit." This is quoted to prove that the single nature is untouched in the new birth, while an entirely new nature, or, rather, new creature, is created, and associated therewith. This view assumes, without proof, the following: —

1. That John uses the term "flesh" in the Pauline sense, which as Meyer says, "is strange to him"; while Cremer, in his Biblico Theological Lexicon, quotes this passage as an instance of John's use of *sarx*, flesh, to signify merely that which "mediates and brings about man's connection with nature." He finds six sh les of meaning to this important word, the

last only embracing the idea of sin. He excludes from this meaning all passages in the four Gospels in which the word occurs.

2. It is assumed that such writers as Weiss, and Julius Müller, are in error when they say that the meaning of Jesus is, "the corporeal birth only produces the corporeal sensual part."

3. There is a confounding of birth with creation out of nothing. "For as generation," says Dr. Whedon, "is a modifying of substance or being, imparting to it a new principle of life, conforming it, as living being, to the likeness of the generator, so regeneration is a modification of the human spirit by the Holy Spirit, conforming the temper of the human to the Holy."

So that that which is born of the Spirit, is the same person as is born of the flesh. He is henceforth endowed with the new quality of spiritual life, instead of spiritual death. The identical man, soul, body, and spirit — "for in the term flesh," says Alford, "is included *every part* of that which is born after the ordinary method of generation "— is born again by the endowment of spiritual life.

What is born again in the view of the imputationist? Not the fallen nature, — that must remain fallen; nothing is born again; but a new man is created *de novo* and put into the believer, who is henceforth to live a dual life, his personality sometimes dwelling under the sway of the old man, and sometimes under the rule of the new. This is not a birth at all. For in a true birth there is a communication of life to non-living matter. So in the spiritual birth there is the impartation of life to a spiritually non-living soul.

4. Our best philosophers say that the only safeguard against materialism is the theory that the soul is created by a direct act of the Creator. This theory would seem to lie at the base of the reasonings of the imputationists on this text, and to afford them an analogy for the absolutely new creation of a spiritual man at the new birth.

Now it is well known in theological circles that there are three theories for the origin of the human spirit, (1) pre-existence from the date of the creation, and waiting to be incarnated, (2) traduction, or derivation from parents, the same as the body, and (3) direct creation at the time of birth, or of generation.

It is not incumbent on me to show which is the true theory. But he who builds on any of these hypotheses must first demonstrate its truth. We assert that the declaration of the imputationists, that a new man is created, not by a transformation and renewal of the old man, but by an immediate creation, rests analogically upon a misunderstood theory respecting the first birth. For this theory is not that of creation absolutely independent of all antecedents, but each soul is created as part of a system which has been dislocated by sin. The Adamic matrix, though marred by sin, being still used in the creation, and not the matrix of a new race.

Well does Augustine say, "Where the Scripture renders no certain testimony, human inquiry must beware of deciding one way or the other."

Let us emerge, then, from this region of speculation into that of common sense. Nicodemus was surely right when he understood that the new birth was a second birth of the same subject. The same man born of the flesh must be born again.

Jesus Himself fully explains the meaning which St. Paul puts into the words, "in Christ," in that wonderful discourse of Christ, in the sixth chapter of John, about the spiritual appropriation of the benefit of His atonement, by sacramentarians, erroneously interpreted as the reception of the Lord's Supper, Christ explains what is signified by being in Him: "He that eateth (continuously) my flesh, and (persistently) drinketh my blood, abideth in me, and I in him." Eternal blessedness is in Him, and is imparted to all who by faith continually appropriate it. With such souls there is a mystical union with Christ, an inter-penetration of Spirit. So long as Jesus abides in the believer, he abides in Him: "Christ in you the hope of glory." This union excludes wilful sin. When this is committed, the union is dissolved. If Christ should continue to dwell in the heart which persists in a course of voluntary transgression of the known law of God, He would become what St. Paul styles, "the minister of sin," and not a destroyer of the works of the devil.

In Mr. Wesley's day, when an un-Scriptural view of the doctrine of imputed righteousness was much preached, he not unfrequently met men who, while claiming to be "perfect in Christ, not in themselves," affirmed that their faith canceled their obligations to obey the Divine law. They might, as they wickedly claimed, violate any or all the ten commandments without being guilty of sin, so long as they maintained faith in Christ. No wonder

Mr. Wesley wrote of such men: "Surely, these are the first-born children of Satan."

The true doctrine of the result of union with Christ, is very truly expressed by Rev. Mr. Sears, of the Unitarian faith: "The atonement brings the believer into such a vital union with Christ as to produce from within, outwardly, not a putative, but a genuine, righteousness."

CHAPTER VI.

THE PLYMOUTH VIEW OF THE ATONEMENT.

THE basis of the doctrine of imputed holiness is that theory of the atonement which represents that Christ Jesus, the sinless Son of God, in whom He was well pleased, was literally identified with sin so as to be "wholly chargeable therewith, that we might be identified and wholly charged with righteousness." This quotation is from Dr. George S. Bishop, who proceeds to say, "The atonement which we preach is one of absolute exchange, that Christ took our place literally — that God regarded and treated Christ as a sinner, and that He regards and treats the believing sinner as Christ. From the moment we believe, God looks upon us as if we were Christ. . . . We then are saved, straight through eternity, by what the Son of God has done in our place. . . . Other considerations have nothing to do with it. It matters nothing what we have been, what we are, or *what we shall be.* From the moment we believe on Christ, we are forever, in God's sight, AS CHRIST. Of course it is involved in this that men are saved, *not by preparing first,* that is, by repenting, and praying, and reading the Bible, and then trusting Christ; nor the converse of this, that is, by trusting Christ first, *and then preparing something* — repentance, reformation, good works — which God will accept; but that sinners are saved irrespective of what they are — how they feel — what they have done — what they hope to do — by trusting on Christ only, that the instant Christ is seen and rested on, the soul's eternity, by God's free promise, and regardless of all character and works, is fixed."

We would call attention to the following points in the above quotation; —

1. Repentance is not necessary to saving faith.

2. Good works, as the fruit of saving faith, and proof of its genuineness, have no place in this scheme of salvation, and are distinctly repudiated; and well they may be, since by the first act of faith, as a bare, intellectual, impenitent apprehension that God punished His Son for our past, present, and future sins, "the soul's eternal salvation, *regardless of conduct and character*, IS FIXED." "What we shall be matters nothing" since we have a through ticket for Heaven. St. James is an impertinence in this scheme of salvation, and his epistle may well be called "strawy."

3. That "God regarded and treated Christ as a sinner"; in other words, that He actually punished His Son because he was guilty of our sins. There was a time in the life of Martin Luther when he sowed the seeds of this error, which produced a sad harvest of antinomianism. He used words which seem not blasphemous, merely because the intention was wanting. "The prophets did foresee in Spirit that Christ

would become the greatest transgressor, murderer, thief, rebel and blasphemer that ever was or can be." "Whatsoever sins I, thou, and we shall have done, or shall do hereafter, they are Christ's own sins, as verily as if He had done them Himself."

We once heard a layman, an ex-president of the Boston Y. M. C. A., assert in a public evangelistic service that "Jesus Christ on the cross was the greatest sinner in the universe!" Such statements are usually attended by the portrayal with terrific distinctness, of the Almighty Father in the act of hurling His thunderbolts, in blasting shocks, down upon the defenceless head of His shrinking and suffering Son.

We indignantly repudiate the monstrous idea that Jesus on the cross was a sinner overwhelmed with the bolts of the Father's personal wrath. What we do affirm is that his sufferings and death were in no sense a punishment, *but a substitute for punishment*, answering the same end, the conservation of God's moral government and the vindication of His holy character while He pardons penitent believers.

The chief proof-text of the doctrine that Christ on the cross was a gigantic sinner, is 2 Cor. v. 21. "For He hath made him to be sin for us, who knew no sin, that we might be made the righteousness of God in Him." This is styled "the sublime equation." Jesus becomes guilty of our sins and suffers their punishment, and His righteousness is henceforth forever reckoned as ours. The exchange of our sin for Christ's righteousness is "absolute."

The common sense exegesis of this text is, that Jesus became of His own free will a *sin-offering* for us, and that this is the meaning of sin in the first clause. This is the interpretation of Augustine, Ambrosiaster, Erasmus, Œcumenius, Vatablus, Cornelius a Lapidis, Piscator, Ritsche, Wolf, Hammond, Michaelis, Rosenmüller, Ewald, Raymond, and others.

It is a remarkable fact that the Hebrew word, *chattath*, is used in the Old Testament by actual count one hundred and sixty times for sin, and one hundred and twelve times for sin-offering. It is very natural that such a mind as Paul's, saturated with the Hebrew Scriptures, should sometimes use the Greek term for sin, *hamartia*, in the sense of sin-offering. So obvious is this usage in Paul's Epistles, that the Revision has twice, at least, translated this term by "sin offering" — Rom. viii. 3; Heb. xiii. 11. We contend that it should be thus rendered in 2 Cor. v. 21.

4. We have insuperable philosophical and ethical difficulties in the way of receiving the statement that the guilt of the race was transferred to Christ. Character is personal, and cannot be transferred. Sin is not an entity, a substance which can be separated from the sinner and be transferred to another and be made an attribute of his character by such a transfer. Sin is the act or state of a sinner, as thought is the act or state of the thinker. Neither can have an essential existence separate from their

personal subject, any more than any attribute can exist separate from its substance.

5. If sin cannot exist in the abstract, it cannot be punished in the abstract. If it cannot be transferred to another, it cannot be punished in another, though one man may voluntarily suffer to save another from punishment.

Hence we repudiate in the interest of sound ethical philosophy and clearness of thought, the following proposition of Dr. Bishop: —

"If the sin of the believing sinner is taken from his shoulders and laid upon the Son of God, then justice, still following after sin, must strike through sin and the person of the Son of God beneath it."

It is a moral axiom that only the guilty can be rightfully punished. If Christ was holy, harmless, undefiled, and separate from sinners, to punish Him would be, not only contrary to all human law, but it would outrage all those God-given moral sentiments on which human law rests. It is in vain that Dr. Bishop seeks for analogies to sustain the monstrous injustice of punishing innocence. He says, "When a father commits a crime, his whole family sink in the social scale, though innocent." Here he confounds the natural consequences of sin with the punishment of sin. Dr. Bishop should show that society universally hangs the innocent family on the same gibbet with the guilty husband and father. Then the case would be analagous.

Many persons use the expression "Christ in the stead of the sinner suffered the punishment of his sin," without subjecting this proposition to that rigid analysis which theological accuracy requires. While it is true that Jesus is our substitute, He is our substitute truly and strictly only in suffering, not in punishment. Sin cannot be punished and pardoned also. This would be a moral contradiction. Sin is conditionally pardoned because Jesus has suffered and died. There is no punishment of sin except in the person of the sinner who neglects so great a Saviour. Sin was not punished on the Cross. Calvary was the scene of wondrous mercy and love, not of wrath and penalty.

Says Dr. Whedon, "Punishment in the strict sense implies the guilt of the sufferer as its correlative. Whenever the sinner and the sufferer are not the same, it is only by an allowable inaccuracy that the suffering can be called punishment. It follows that it is not strictly accurate to say that Christ was punished, or that he truly suffered the punishment of sin."

But this inaccuracy is no longer "allowable" when it is made the basis of the doctrine of imputed holiness, which tramples the holy law of God under foot, and flings its obligations to the winds on the plea of an inalienable standing in Christ, in whom, despite my wallowing in fleshly lusts, I am seen to be as holy as He is holy.

6. But the ethical difficulties thicken as we continue our examination of this view of the atonement.

A Limited Atonement

Is the inevitable outcome of the doctrine that sin was punished on the cross. Whose sin? If it be answered, that of the whole human race, then universalism emerges, for God cannot in justice punish sin twice. It must be, then, that the sins of the elect only were punished. Hence at the bottom, this system of doctrine rests upon the tenet of a particular, in distinction from a universal atonement. The fact that this basis is not avowed, and that the terminology of hyper-predestinarianism, such as "the elect," "the reprobates," "special call," "irresistible grace," "perseverance of the saints," and salvation by "Divine Sovereignty," is studiously avoided, makes this system of doctrine still more dangerous, because these offensive features are concealed with Jesuitical cunning. We cannot resist the suspicion that this is designed, so as to make it palatable to those educated in the Arminian faith, in order to catch them with guile. Some unreflective Arminians are thus unawares entrapped into the reception of that unmitigated scheme of doctrine which Christendom is almost universally shaking off.

In our first interview with Mr. Darby, we asked what was his view of election founded on the foreseen, free, acceptance of the conditions of salvation, repentance toward God, and faith in Jesus Christ. His reply was that "an election, grounded upon reasons, would destroy the sovereignty of God, and that no act of the creature, no foreseen faith in Christ, conditioned election."

CHAPTER VII.

ETERNAL LIFE NON-FORFEITABLE.

In two instances Jesus speaks of everlasting life as a present possession: "He that heareth (continually) my words hath everlasting life" (John v. 24); "He that believeth (perseveringly) on me hath everlasting life" (John vi. 47).

The reader of the Greek Testament sees at a glance the condition expressed in the present tense of the verb "heareth" and "believeth." If these conditions are fulfilled, the new life inspired by the first act of evangelical faith becomes everlasting. This is the common sense view. If this faith, at any point of probation, lapses, the life expires. That everlasting life once begun can be lost, is no more a contradiction in terms than the Jew's forfeiture of the land which God gave to them for "an everlasting possession" (Gen. xvii. 8), nor the seed of Phineas losing "the everlasting priesthood," nor the Israelites breaking "the everlasting covenant" (Is. xxiv. 5), and finding out Jehovah's "breach of promise" (Num. xiv. 34). Hymeneus and Philetus forfeited the everlasting heritage of believers by "making shipwreck of faith and a good conscience."

We infer, therefore, that the words "hath everlasting life," were never designed as a non-forfeitable insurance policy, giving an unconditional and inalienable right to the rewards of Heaven. They are a compendious expression for the spiritual life already inspired, which is destined to become everlasting if its conditions are fulfilled through the whole of our probation.

A Soul Born of God can never be Unborn.

An abuse of figurative language is a stronghold of religious error. Antinomianism seizes upon "the new birth," "the being born again," "a child or son of God," and presses these phrases into a proof of an unchangeable acceptance with God, however grossly sinful the once regenerate person may afterwards become. J. Fletcher thus points out the fallacy in this reasoning: "According to the oriental style, a follower of wisdom is called 'a son of wisdom'; and one that deviates from her path, 'a son of folly'; a wicked man is called 'a son of Belial, a child of the wicked one, and a child of the devil.' But when he turns from wicked works, by faith, he becomes a child of God. Hence the passing from the ways of Satan to the ways of God was naturally called *conversion* and a *new birth*. Hence some divines, who, like Nicodemus, carnalize the expressions *new birth, child of God*, and *son of God*, assert, that if men who once walked in God's ways turn back, even into adultery, murder, and incest, they are still God's *dear people* and *pleasant children*, in the Gospel sense of the words. They ask, "Can a man be a child of God to-day, and a child of the devil to-morrow?

ETERNAL LIFE NON-FORFEITABLE. 135

Can he be born this week, and unborn the next?" And with these questions they as much think they have overthrown the doctrine of holiness, and one-half of the Bible, as honest Nicodemus supposed he had demolished the doctrine of regeneration, and stopped our Lord's mouth, when he said, "Can a man enter the second time into his mother's womb and be born?"

The question would be easily answered, if, setting aside the oriental mode of speech, they simply asked, "May one who has 'ceased to do evil' and learned to do well *to-day*, cease to do well and learn to do evil *to-morrow?* To this we could directly reply, If the dying thief, the Philippian jailor, and multitudes of Jews, in one day went over from the *sons of folly* to the *sons of wisdom*, where is the absurdity of saying they could measure the same way back again in one day, and draw back in the horrid womb of sin as easily as Satan drew back into rebellion, Adam into disobedience, David into adultery, Solomon into idolatry, Judas into treason, and

Ananias and Sapphira into covetousness? When Peter had shown himself a blessed son of heavenly wisdom, by confessing Jesus Christ, did he even stay till the next day to become a son of folly by following the "wisdom which is earthly, sensual, and devilish"? Was not our Lord directly obliged to rebuke him with utmost severity, by saying, "Get thee behind me, Satan"?

A Sheep can never become a Goat.

Here is another Antinomian abuse of figures. In the day of judgment the human race stand separate — the sheep and the goats. It is said that since a sheep can never become a goat, because of the law of the invariability of species, so one once called by Christ a sheep can never become a goat. But this logic proves too much. Can a goat ever, by any power divine, become a sheep? Can a sinner ever become a saint if it is impossible for a saint ever to become an incorrigible sinner? Yet multitudes, who live in sins cannot hurt them, so there is no cause of fear in their sins committed. Sins are but scarecrows and bugbears to frighten ignorant children, but men of understanding see they are counterfeit things. If we tell believers, except they walk thus and thus holily, and do these and these good works, God will be angry with them, we abuse the Scriptures, undo what Christ has done, injure believers, and tell God lies to His face. All our righteousness is filthy, full of menstruosity, the highest kind of filthiness;—even what is the Spirit's must be involved within that which is man's own, under the general notion of *doing*."

"It is a soft and easy doctrine to bid men sit still and believe, as if God would translate them to heaven upon their couches! Christ expects that those who have grace should put forth the utmost power thereof in laboring after the salvation He has purchased for them." "So work with that earnestness, constancy, and unweariness in well doing, as if thy works alone were able to justify and save thee; and so absolutely depend and rely upon the merits of Christ for justification and salvation, as if thou never hadst performed one act of obedience in all thy life. This is the right Gospel frame of obedience, so to work as if we were only to be saved by our own merits; and withal so to rest on the merits of Christ, as if we had never wrought anything. It is a difficult thing to give to each of these its due in practice. When we work, we are apt to neglect Christ; and when we rely on Christ we are apt to neglect working. But that Christian has got the right art of obedience who can mingle these two together; who can with one hand 'work the works of God,' and yet, at the same time, lay fast hold on the merit of Jesus Christ. Let this Antinomian principle be forever rooted out of the minds of men, that our working is derogatory to Christ's work. 'He gave himself for us, that He might redeem us from all iniquity, and purify to Himself a peculiar people, ZEALOUS OF GOOD WORKS.'"

MODERN ANTINOMIANISM.

We quote from modern writers essentially the same doctrines as those taught by Dr. Crisp, only there is apparently a shrinking from the frank statement of their logical outcome. There is rather an attempt to draw a vail over those inferences which old Antinomianism plainly avowed. In this particular, the old is less dangerous than the new.

We turn to McIntosh's Notes on various books of the Bible, a series of diffuse annotations highly esteemed by D. L. Moody and many other evangelists: "The very moment in which a soul is born again, — born from above, and sealed by the Holy Ghost, — he is incorporated into the body of Christ. He can no longer view himself as a solitary individual — an independent person — an isolated atom; he is a member of a body, just as the hand or foot is a member of the human body." "There are two grand links in Christianity, which, though very intimately connected, are perfectly distinct; namely, the link of eternal life, and the link of personal communion. *The former never can be snapped by anything*, the latter can be snapped in a moment, by the weight of a feather." It seems that a sin as light as a feather can suspend communion, while the violation of every one of the ten commandments, over and over again, can never snap the link of eternal life! Comforting indeed to the backslider! His fear that he may at last be filled with his own ways, are groundless. "Beholders many faults may find; but, as regards our standing, our God sees us only in the comeliness of Christ; we are perfect in Him. When God looks at His people, He beholds in them His own workmanship; and it is to the glory of His holy name, and to the praise of His salvation, that not a blemish should be seen on those who are His — those whom He, in sovereign grace, has made His own. His character, His name, His glory, and the perfection of

His work, are all involved in the standing of those with whom He has linked Himself." Thus it would seem that David's workmanship, in making himself an adulterer and a murderer, is utterly ignored as a blemish. While in Uriah's bed his standing as perfectly holy is absolute. "We must never measure the standing by the state, but always judge the state by the standing. To lower the standing because of the state, is to give the death-blow to all progress in practical Christianity." That is, we must never judge the tree by the fruit, but always the fruit by the tree. If a crab scion, grafted on a golden pippin, still produces crab-apples, we must aver that they are golden pippins, because the crab has a golden pippin standing. "The people of God are seen only in 'the vision of the Almighty'—seen as He sees them, without spot or wrinkle, or any such thing—all their deformities hidden from view—all His comeliness seen upon them." "He hath not beheld iniquity in Jacob, neither hath he seen perverseness in Israel." The enemy may say, "There is iniquity and perverseness there all the while." "Yes; but who can make Jehovah behold it, when He Himself has been pleased to blot it all out as a thick cloud for His name's sake?" "God will never reverse His decision as to what His people are as to standing."

This is the comment on the shameless licentiousness of Israel on the plains of Moab, with the women of Midian. Their standing is still the same as it was when the prophet stood on Pisgah. "It reminds us of the opening and close of 2 Cor. xii. In the former we have the *positive standing* of the Christian; in the latter, the *possible state* into which he may fall, if not watchful. That shows us a "man in Christ" capable of being caught up into Paradise at any moment. This shows us saints of God capable of plunging into all manner of sin and folly." Of course the plunge into the cesspool has not the least damaging effect on their clean standing in Christ. These quotations are from McIntosh on Numbers.

CHAPTER VIII.

HOLINESS IMPUTED.

THERE is much confused and erroneous thinking and teaching on the subject of imputed righteousness and imputed holiness. Some are confounding the two, and teaching that the only holiness possible to us in this world is the robe of Christ's righteousness thrown around hearts inherently impure. In the interest of clear thought and Christian purity, we invite the reader to a discussion of the radical distinction between imputed righteousness and imputed holiness. The term "impute," literally signifies "to think to," to reckon one thing belongs to another when it really does not. In the Revision it is superseded by the word "reckon."

We define righteousness in man to be conformity to the Divine law, and holiness conformity to the Divine nature.

Jesus Christ is both righteous and holy. These qualities are personal, inherent, and untransferable. But in addition to His personal righteousness He has a mediatorial righteousness, the merit of His passive obedience, labors, sacrifices, sufferings, death, and high-priestly intercessions. Now, although the phrase, "the imputation of Christ's righteousness," or "Christ's imputed righteousness," is not found in the Bible, the doctrine itself is found in the epistles of Paul unfolded extendedly, and it is hinted at in the Gospels when Jesus speaks of giving His life for the world, or as a ransom for many. But it is always His mediatorial, and not His personal righteousness. The absolute necessity of this imputation in the scheme of redemption, arises from the fact that one past sin produces an eternal disconformity to the Divine law, so that the Lawgiver cannot treat us as if we had never sinned without violating the truth of history, and cheating the law of its demands. Hence pardon and salvation would be impossible under the reign of strict and unbending law. But here comes in the mediatorial righteousness of Christ to all who plead it as the ground of justification, so that God can be just and the justifier of him who believeth. In other words, there is a constructive, not to say fictitious, conformity, to the law, now possible through faith in the merits of Christ. Otherwise, law would be forever against us. The necessity of this scheme of imputation lies in the fact that God Himself cannot change the past. It is a record absolutely inerasible.

But when God wishes to make men holy, or bring them into conformity to His own nature, there is no such inerasible record in the way. Justification is a work done for us, and has reference to the past; sanctification is a work wrought in us, and always has respect to the present. Hence, imputation of holiness is not necessary. In fact, in the very nature of things, it is impossible. There can be no such thing as vicarious character, for character is the sum total of what we ourselves are. There may be a vicarious assumption of another's debt; there cannot be a vicarious assumption of another's character. Hence, holiness must be personal, inherent, inwrought and imparted by the power of the Holy Spirit, procured by the same atonement by which it is possible for us, through faith, to be conformed to the Divine law, or savingly adjusted to an inerasible, sinful record.

In Christ.

The phrase "in Christ" is perpetually quoted as a proof-text to sustain the doctrine of imputed holiness, a quality not imparted to us, being inwrought by the Holy Spirit and ever afterwards existing inherently in the believer; but an attribute of Jesus Christ regarded by God as belonging to Christians, even when they are unholy in character and wicked in conduct.

The theory is that Jesus Christ is standing to-day in the presence of the Father as a specimen and representative of glorified humanity, and that faith in Him so intimately unites us with Him, that all His personal excellencies become ours in such a sense as to excuse us if we lack them. It is said that the first act of faith eternally incorporates us into the glorified person of Christ, so that whatever sin we may commit afterwards we incur no condemnation.

Says Fletcher: "People, it seems, may now be 'in Christ,' without being 'new creatures,' and 'new creatures' without casting 'old things' away. They may be God's children without God's image; and 'born of the Spirit' without 'the fruit of the Spirit.'"

The favorite proof-text of this piece of rank Antinomianism is Rom. viii. 1: "There is therefore now no condemnation to them that are in Christ Jesus," with special attention called to the omission by the critical MSS. and the Revised Version, of the limiting clause: "who walk not after the flesh, but after the spirit." Over this omission the imputationists rejoice, as if it unanswerably demonstrated the truth of their doctrine, that God, seeing the believer only in Christ, beholds no sin in him, even when he has wilfully and flagrantly transgressed the known law. They fail to note that the same limiting clause stands in the fourth verse unquestioned by the critics.

Hence their assertion that the flesh is a sinful state which does not in the least damage our perfect standing in Christ, in whom the carnally-minded believer is as holy as the Son of God Himself. It is said that "the standing is never to be judged by the state, but the state by the standing." The New Testament Scriptures relied on as proofs of this doctrine are those in which our faith is imputed for righteousness. The error is in failing to notice that this refers to the forgiveness of sins, and not to the character after justification.

Another mistake is in not distinguishing between the sum total of Christ's merits, called His mediatorial righteousness, and His own personal righteousness, which is not transferable. Character is personal and unimputable.

Another constantly recurring Scripture is the expression, "in Christ"— used to prove an actual incorporation into His Person. We take up our pen to examine these words. They are not found in the four Gospels nor in the Acts of the Apostles. They are Pauline, being used only by Paul, except in 1 Pet. iii. 16; v. 14. The words, "in the Lord," are peculiar to Paul also. Elsewhere they are found only in Rev. xiv. 13. What does Paul mean by these phrases?

1. He does not mean incorporation into the glorified Person of Christ, for he always (except in 1 Cor. xv. 18 —"asleep in Jesus") avoids His purely personal name, Jesus, never saying "in Jesus," but he always adds one of His titular names, Christ, or Lord.* "In Christ,"

* On "truth as it is in Jesus," see Meyer. Eph. iv. 21. Quote Meyer and Bengel.

or "in the Lord," must mean, then, some intimate relation to His official work.

2. What this relation is will be seen when we observe that while Luke and Peter use the term "Christian," Paul never used it, but uses the more vivid phrase, "in Christ." Let us now examine a favorite text of the imputationists — 1 Cor. i. 2: "To them that are sanctified in Christ Jesus." We heartily endorse the comment of Meyer, "the greatest exegete of the nineteenth century": "In Christ — namely, in His redemptive work, of which Christians have become, and continue to be, partakers, by means of justifying faith (Eph. i. 4; Heb. x. 10)." In the fourth verse, Meyer's note on "in Christ," is "in your fellowship with Christ." His paraphase of the thirtieth verse, "But of Him are ye in Christ Jesus, who of God is made unto us wisdom, and righteousness, and sanctification, and redemption," is the following: "But truly it is God's work that ye are Christians, and so partakers of the greatest Divine

blessings, that none of you should in any way boast himself save only in God." Rom. xvi. 7; " In Christ before me " — Christians before me. Rom. xvi. 10; "Approved in Christ"— *i. e.,* says Meyer, " the tried Christian." 2 Cor. v. 17; " If any man is in Christ " a Christian, says the same annotator.

Cremer, in his Biblico-Theological Lexicon, enumerates forty-eight texts where this phrase is used with the above meaning, such as "weak in Christ" and "babes in Christ," for feeble Christians; "growing up in Christ," for an advancing Christian; "perfect in Christ," for a believer fully sanctified, or, in the words of Meyer, "perfect as a Christian, in respect to the whole Christian nature." " Holy in Christ " is a phrase foreign to New Testament diction. The general meaning of the words, "in the Lord," is discipleship to the Lord Jesus, as in Rom. xvi. 2: "which are in the Lord"; 1 Cor. vii. 39; " To be married in the Lord"; *i. e.,* to a disciple of the Lord Jesus.

The expressions "in Christ" and "in the Lord" are the Pauline way of denoting a saving relation to the Son of God, a union with Him by faith, a union which ceases when the faith decays. It is quite probable that St. Paul's use of this peculiar idiom is an amplification of the words of Christ, "If ye abide in Me," in His parable of the true vine, John xv. 1-7. That He does not here speak of an inseparable and eternal incorporation into His person, is evident from these words: "Every branch in Me that beareth not fruit, He taketh away." That this taking away is no mere temporary break in the saving relation to Christ, but an eternal cutting off, will be seen by reading the sixth verse: "If a man abide not in Me, he is cast forth as a branch and is withered, and men gather them and cast them into the fire, and they are burned." This solemn and expressive language is utterly meaningless, if the phrase "in Me," or "in Christ," means an inalienable standing in Christ wholly independent of one's real character. Those modern champions of imputed holiness, and opponents of inwrought personal purity, the Plymouth brethren, find their air-castle rudely swept away when these words of Jesus are directed against it. A branch in the true vine may die and be sundered and burned.

This is a complete answer to the words of Rev. John Darby to the writer, that "believers are parts of the glorified Person of Jesus Christ, who does not walk about in Heaven dropping His fingers and toes by self-mutilation, but retains every part and particle of His body forever." The revised version, in Eph. v. 30, omits "of His flesh and of His bones," and thus removes a seeming proof-text for the incorporation theory.

3. This paper would not be complete if we did not refer to the objective use, by St Paul, of the phrase "in Christ," as representing, not the peculiar union of the believing subject, but the blessings of redemption included in Jesus. In this Apostle's writings, the idiom, "in

Christ," has a Godward, or objective meaning, when he describes the provisions for salvation embodied in the Person and work of the Son, and a manward, or subjective meaning, when he speaks of the believer as appropriating those provisions. As a specimen of the objective use, we quote Rom. vi. 23: "But the free gift of God is eternal life in Christ Jesus our Lord" (R. V.). See also Rom. viii. 2, 39; 1 Cor. i. 4 (R. V.); 2 Cor. v. 19; Gal. ii. 4, iii. 14 (R. V.); Eph. i. 3, ii. 6. 7 (R. V.), iii. 11, iv. 32 (R. V.); Phil. ii. 5; 2 Tim ii. 10. In all these passages Jesus Christ is presented as God's treasury of grace and salvation. In examining these texts the reader will be impressed with the superior precision of the revisors in their translation of the preposition "*en*," in. There are instances in which this Pauline idiom embraces both the subjective and the objective, notably Rom. vi. 11, "Alive unto God in Christ Jesus" (R. V.). Here the believer appropriates the life that exists in Jesus.

Writers in classical Greek exemplify only the objective use of "*en.*" Thus Sophocles: "I indeed am saved wholly in thee"; Hesiod: "Whether Athens shall be enslaved or freed is now in thee"; says Homer: "Complete victory is in the immortal gods."

But St. Paul's use of "in," as expressing the activity of the subject appropriating Christ, from the very nature of the case, has no verbal parallels in profane Greek.

In conclusion, we aver that it is just as reasonable to interpret 1 John v. 19, "The whole world lieth in the evil one" (R. V.), as meaning that the whole world is in itself inherently saintly, but by imputation is wicked in the evil one, as it is to say that the best estate of believers on earth is to be inherently impure, while by imputation they are spotless in Christ. According to the testimony of that cosmopolitan evangelist, Wm. Taylor, imputed holiness, enrobing cherished vileness, is a favorite fiction of the pagans of India. A fakir in his presence professing spotless holiness, was rebuked by the crowd as a liar, a cheat, and an adulterer. Admitting the truth of these charges, the fakir triumphantly exclaimed: "I am vile in myself, but perfectly holy in Vishnu." *

To be holy with a retention of the old man, would be an untruth and a flat contradiction (Meyer on Eph. iv. 21.)

* The Plymouth Brethren established a mission among the Canarese in India which afterwards was turned over to the Methodists, who found the converts so morally perverted by antinomian doctrines that it became necessary to translate "Antinomianism Revived" into the Canarese in order to save the mission from a demoralization worse than Hinduism. The translation was made by Rev. Ira A. Richards, M.A., as a labor of love for the souls of his deluded fellow-men. It is published in Madras by the M. E. Publishing House, 1896.

CHAPTER IX.

PLYMOUTH ESCHATOLOGY, OR LAST THINGS.

THIS school of theologians dwells at great length upon the future history of Christianity as it is unrolled to their anointed eyes in prophecy. They differ from the ordinary Adventists, inasmuch as they believe in a second and a third coming of Christ — the first *for* the saints, and the second *with* them. In the first, Christ will not appear to the world, which will be in utter ignorance of that great event. At some day — not fixed in the Plymouth scheme, but near at hand — Jesus will come down with noiseless footfall, like a thief, and raise the righteous dead, and change the righteous living, and snatch them all up in the twinkling of an eye; and no unbeliever will notice any disturbance in the graveyard or see his believing wife or child slip out of this world into the glorified state. He will miss them, and wonder where they are. This "rapture of the saints" is foretold in 1 Thess. iv. 17. But in the 16th verse there are three words indicating noise — a shout, the voice of the archangel, and the trump of God. But Plymouth exegesis easily explains this little objection. Dr. Tyng, the younger, says the shout is, in the Greek, a command, heard only by the living and the dead saints. The invisibleness of the resurrection and the rapture are argued from Christ's resurrection, and the translation of Enoch and Elijah, all of which were unobserved by the wicked world.

Again, all you know about the burglar is that your treasures are gone. You did not hear his wool-shod feet; you did not see his form while he was gliding about your bed. All that ordinary readers have seen in the simile, "as a thief," is the suddenness and unexpectedness of His advent. The Plymouth brethren add the perfect secrecy of His coming, work, and departure, thus making the comparison teach more than Christ ever intended.

The saints caught up into the air will be reviewed by Christ with a view to the distribution of offices under His millennial reign. It seems that the question of patronage meets Christ at the opening of His kingdom on earth, just as it vexes every new president of the United States. But Jesus will have no hostile senate to conciliate. His civil service appointments will be made according to merit, after a rigid examination. In this way the *works* of the saints, but not their *persons*, will come to judgment. The question of their personal relation to the divine government was forever adjusted when they put forth the first act of faith in Christ. All the thrones, presidencies, governorships, secretaryships, judgeships, mayoralties, etc., down to the office of justice of the peace and constable, in all nations, will then be considered as vacant. The time occupied by this inquest into the works of the saints and their assignment to office, is supposed to occupy about seven years. Then when the state of the future millennial administration is made up satisfactorily to all concerned, the King descends with all His retinue of saints in all the pomp and majesty of royalty, impressing every beholder with awe and wonder. Now He *appears*. (See App.)

But the world to which He comes is in a sorry condition. The devil and Antichrists have driven rough-shod over the earth in the absence of the saints, and all the woes of the book of Revelation have been experienced; all the events of that book after the third chapter take place—the trumpets, the seals, and the vials.

By this time the world is sadly in need of a universal king, to bring order out of chaos. King Jesus makes Jerusalem His capital, and sends His appointees to their respective countries to enter upon their various offices. Perhaps St. Paul may mount the throne of Great Britain and the Indies, or become the President of the United States, without the bother of an electoral college. The Jews are all going to wheel into line by sudden conversion like that of Saul of Tarsus, and become Christ's right-hand men — the inner circle nearest the throne. They will become the great missionary agency, travelling through all lands, and preaching Christ, the Jews' Messiah and the world's Saviour. Satan will be bound in his prison-house a thousand years, and the Gospel, which was a failure for eighteen hundred years, will now begin its real conquest of the world. In fact, it never was Christ's design that the world should be converted through the great commission, "Go ye into all the world and preach," etc. That was designed only to keep alive on earth a testimony for Christ, not to inaugurate a victory.

In the absence of Satan, and in the presence of so many Hebrew Christian missionaries steaming over every sea and traversing all lands, impelled by their new-born zeal for the Nazarene, the work of conversion goes on very rapidly, and a nation is born in a day. At the close of the thousand years there is a review of the nations, and the inquiry is made how they have treated Christ's brethren, the Jewish evangelists. This review of the nations — not of individuals — in a general judgment, is described in Matt. xxv. 31-46. If you wish to embarrass a Plymouth brother, ask him to expound the whole passage, carrying through it from beginning to end the idea that nations, and not individuals of the human family, are there judged and eternally sentenced. The brother's embarrassment will be painful, and his makeshifts will be pitiable.

At the end of the millennium Satan is loosed for a season and makes sad havoc with the converts made in his incarceration. He raises an army and encompasses the camp of the saints, is conquered, and, with Antichrist, is cast into the lake of fire, the latter being a living man.

Finally, the wicked dead are raised and

judged according to the description of the judgment of the dead, in Rev. xx. 12–15. To make out that only the wicked dead are judged, the Book of Life which is brought into the judgment is assumed to be blank. This is a very violent assumption, as the reader of the passsge will see.

After the sentence of the wicked dead, come the new heavens and the new earth — the eternal abode of the saints, if I can make out the meaning of the Plymouth doctrine on this point.

The effect of this teaching is, first, to belittle the Christian agencies now in operation by asserting that they are inadequate to the conversion of the world. Secondly, it gives a Jewish and highly materialistic turn to the kingdom of Christ, and leads to a depreciation of the spiritual manifestation of Christ by the Comforter in this life. Thirdly, it calls off the attention from the great saving truths of the Gospel, and leads believers to dwell upon airy and baseless speculations, and profitless argumentation. Fourthly, unless the laws of mind are all changed in this generation, we predict from the history of Adventism in past ages, that the Plymouth Brethren will soon begin to fix a definite time for the Advent, which will be followed by disappointment and all the moral and spiritual disasters of Millerism.

PESSIMISM.

One of the most depressing doctrines of the Pre-Millenarians, especially of the "Brethren," is the hopelessness of the world under the dispensation of the Holy Spirit. They always and everywhere assume that this dispensation is a stupendous failure. "From the Cross to the Second Advent there is nothing but a parenthesis." I shudder at the disrespect which is thus shown to the Paraclete, the personal successor to the risen Lord Jesus.

It is, moreover, an imputation of a lack of goodness on the part of God to let the world wax worse and worse, and generation after generation go down to hell, who might have been saved or their existence prevented by the earlier coming of Christ to set up His earthly kingdom, converting the Jews in a day, and, through them, converting the Gentiles in a wholesale way by sheer omnipotence. But if the world is growing better under a purer and more widely preached Gospel, there is a merciful reason for the delay of the second coming of Christ to wind up the period of human history by judging the quick and the dead and assigning them to eternal destinies.

THE PARABLE OF THE LEAVEN.

Every one of the Plymouth expositors, without exception, attempts, by a wonderful exegesis of the parable, to show that the world is steadily and certainly going to the bad. Here is the exposition: "The leaven does not mean the Gospel; it everywhere, in the language of the Spirit of God, which is always beautifully consistent with itself, means something evil. In twenty places, we have mention of leaven, and it always denotes evil. Into the 'three measures of meal,' not into *the world*, not into *society at large* — no, but into the new, *unleavened lump — into the church* — a leavenlike mystery of iniquity is introduced by the 'woman,' the seducer, the mother of harlots. The very *hiding* of it looks suspicious. Could this mean the public preaching of the Gospel? The whole lump — sad announcement! — was to be leavened. Has not this announcement been fulfilled?" Then follows a dismal picture of Christianity, painted with a brush dipped in the blackness of darkness, ending with this question, "Is there one single Christian here whose garments are not soiled, in whose heart '*leaven*,' in one form or another, is not working?" *

Let us now turn to Matt. xiii. 31–33. The mustard seed certainly represents the kingdom

* Eight Lectures on Prophecy.

of heaven in this one aspect, its inherent self-developing power from a small vital germ. The leaven just as certainly represents, not a foreign, corrupting principle thrust into the kingdom of heaven, but that kingdom itself in another aspect, its power to penetrate and assimilate a foreign mass. As the yeast transforms the heavy and indigestible dough into light and wholesome bread, so does the Gospel transform wicked hearts. For the leaven has its good side as well as its bad, and to this good use the Gospel is compared. This is the traditional explanation of this parable, which is certainly full of good sense.

Let us examine the Plymouth view. The meal is the church. This is a pure assumption. The form of words, in both parables, is the same. The kingdom is like a grain of mustard-seed, and like leaven. If it is like it in its progress of corruption and deterioration, surely "there is," as Alford well says, "an end of all the blessing and healing influence of the Gospel on the world."

The Grain of Mustard-seed.

Not content with a pessimistic perversion of the parable of the leaven, they attempt to foist an entirely new meaning upon the preceding parable. The mustard-plant grows in order to attract to its branches the carrion-eating birds, "the vulture, the cormorant, the night-owl and the bat." These "unclean birds" typify the gross abominations predicted by Christ as nesting in His Church. But what is the proof? The Lord himself tells us, in the previous parable, who are the "fowls" or "birds of the air"; for it is the same word that is used in both places. "Then cometh *the wicked one* and catcheth away that which was sown in his heart." Therefore, the birds which picked up the farmer's seed scattered on the sidewalk, were not clean, grain-eating birds, such as pigeons and doves, but were vultures and owls! "Thus the kingdom of heaven, as it purports to be, or nominal, national Christianity, becomes a vast and monstrous worldly system."

A meaning utterly different from that intended by the great Teacher is read into His words by a style of reasoning which would pervert and subvert the whole Bible, if it were universally applied. Yet this sophistry is eagerly swallowed by those who desire to prove that the world is on the down grade, nearing the brink of destruction, and the church is crowded with a plethora of sins, and is so far gone in wickedness as to be past praying for, and deserves nothing but vilification and denunciation by all true lovers of Christ's appearing. We do not wonder that "the Brethren" are all come-outers after they have accepted this interpretation of these two parables.

Probation Closed in Adam's Fall.

One is surprised, in reading Plymouth theology, by the declaration made by all the writers that human probation closed with fall of Adam.

The idea seems to be that, since legal justification is impossible to the fallen race, that " the era of probation has been finally foreclosed." "The Holy Spirit," says Dr. R. Anderson, "has not come to re-open the question of sin and righteousness and judgment, but to convince the world that it is closed forever." How different is this from St. Peter's exordium at Cæsarea! "Of a truth I perceive that God is no respecter of persons; but in every nation he that feareth Him and worketh righteousness is accepted with Him." This looks like probation on the plane of natural theology, the religion of the conscience. St. Paul seems to endorse Peter's doctrine in Rom. ii. 6–16. No one can study this whole passage without admitting that pagans, without the law, and without the knowledge of the Gospel, are being put to the test by God to show whether they have the spirit of faith; *i. e.*, the disposition to grasp Christ, the object of faith, were He revealed to them; and the purpose of righteousness, *i. e.*, the disposition to walk by the perfect law, were it disclosed to them. This I call probation. I do not see how the "Brethren" can, by any possible theodice, justify God for bringing countless millions of fallen beings into existence in a state of hopelessness implied in probation "forever foreclosed."

If they mean to say that no man since Adam's expulsion from Eden is under the dispensation of mere justice expressed in law, but that all men ever since that sad event have been under justice tempered by mercy, as revealed in the Gospel, and that they are still on probation but under changed conditions, no one would object. For all sound theologians reckon the Gospel dispensation as dating from the promise, "The seed of the woman shall bruise the serpent's head."

A little reflection will show that the denial of human probation is a logical antecedent of the negation of a general judgment of the race. If the race is not on trial in probation, there is no need for such a day. The two errors are yoke-fellows. They stumble and fall together.

But the doctrine of the general judgment at the end of the world, strongly implying, as it does, that all men are now on probation, must be explained away by the Brethren, for the two doctrines cannot both be true. Let us see how they succeed.

Never under Condemnation.

The constant assertion of the Plymouth Brethren is, that a person, once "in Christ," by a momentary act of faith, is forever removed from the possibility of Divine, judicial disapproval. Let us examine their Scriptural proofs.

Romans viii. 1, as translated in the Revision, which omits the last clause, is frequently cited as an absolute and unconditional deliverance from present and future condemnation. I have elsewhere shown that this exemption is conditioned on the relative clause, in the fourth verse, "who walk not after the flesh, but after the Spirit," *i.e.*, while we walk thus. This conditioning clause has as much force in the fourth verse as it would have had in the first.

John iii. 18, "He that believeth on Him is not condemned." Here the word believeth is in the Greek, in the present tense, which denotes a continuous state of faith. He who believes perseveringly is not, at any point of his faithful life, under condemnation.

The same explanation applies to Rom. viii. 33–39. The "we" and "us" of this passage refer, not to all men, but to persevering believers. In Gal. iii. 13, "Christ redeemed us from the curse of the law." The persons included in "us" are fully described in the eleventh and twelfth verses, those who constantly live by a faith which bears the fruit of obedience. "The just shall live by faith."

THE SAINTS WILL NOT BE JUDGED IN THE LAST DAY.

This doctrine is really included in the preceding. The word for "condemnation" is often translated "judgment" in the Revision. The great proof-text of the "Brethren" is John v. 24: "Verily, verily, I say unto you, He that heareth my word, and believeth him that sent Me, hath eternal life, and cometh not into judgment, but has passed out of death into life." (R. V.) Here the "judgment" evidently means the condemnatory side of the great tribunal. The life begins with the believing, and continues, and becomes eternal on the condition of faith persisted in through human probation. As Dean Alford well says: "Where the faith is, the possession of eternal life is; and where the one remits, the other is forfeited. But here the faith is set before us as an *enduring* faith, and its effects described *in their completion*." (See Eph. i. 19, 20.)

In all of God's promises of eternal life to the righteous, there is an implied condition which is sometimes expressed, as in Heb. iii. 6, 14, 2 Pet. i. 10, 11, Rev. xxii. 14 (R. V.)

The grand reason why the saints will not be judged, lies in the fact that their sins were judged on the cross, and condemned once for all; and the believer need not have any concern about his sins past, present and future, since in the sight of God they are blotted out forever. Very comforting doctrine, this! The future immoralities of the saints are annihilated by the blood of Christ; and we are the saints. We have a certificate of our heavenly standing signed and sealed by the Holy Spirit. This is my paid-up, non-forfeiting insurance policy. An occasional outburst of unholy tempers or indulgence in the lusts of the flesh may becloud my communion for an hour, but they cannot damage my standing in Christ, or vitiate my title to life everlasting. If one should fall into habitual sin, "he only sleeps." As sleep does not affect the validity of a man's title-deeds to his farms, so spiritual sleep the most profound does not damage my title to the skies. Precious doctrine! Who is so unbelieving as not to fall in love with it at first sight, especially if he be a periodical Christian, and is most of the time at the aphelion?

But on what is this doctrine built? On these two words — *in Christ*. Let us hear what Jesus Himself says: "If any man abide not in Me, he is cast forth as a branch, and is withered, and men gather them, and cast them into the fire, and they are burned." The minuteness of this description of a branch of the true Vine, once vitalized by its sap; the pictorial and impressive portrayal, just before the apostasy of Judas, of these five particulars, — the withering, the cutting off, the gathering, the casting into the fire, and the burning, — have an import of deep and awful solemnity, disclosing, as they do, that the most intimate unity with Christ, in probation, does not shut out the possibility of a perverse use of our free agency, entailing eternal perdition.

A Judgment of Persons and a Judgment of Works.

Before leaving this topic, we should notice the Plymouth distinction between a judgment of persons and a judgment of works. They teach that the persons of believers were judged at the cross, and they were acquitted once for all. Their works are to be reviewed by Christ, not to determine the question of destiny to heaven or to hell, but to decide on each one's amount of rewards. This, they say, is not properly called a judgment. But the Scriptures make no such distinction. We are to be judged and assigned to a destiny of bliss or woe, according to the deeds done in the body.

When a criminal act is condemned, the criminal actor is condemned. Human courts know nothing of a fancied judgment of works aside from the worker. The purpose for which they administer law is to reach persons by their judgments.

A radical error in Plymouth ethics seems to be a forgetfulness that a moral agent is a unit incapable of division into parts, as the old man and the new man, the person and the works, one of which segments may be innocent, and the other guilty. This error we have refuted in the discussion of the two natures.

The General Judgment Denied.

The General Judgment at the last day is very stoutly denied by the "Brethren," as may be inferred from the last paragraph. If the reader wishes to confound them and make them writhe in pain, ask them to explain St. Paul's words in Rom. xiv. 10-12: "For we shall all stand before the judgment seat of Christ (God — Rev. Ver.) For it is written, as I live, saith the Lord, to me every knee shall bow, and every tongue shall confess to God. So then each one of us shall give account of himself to God." Here the "Brethren" must choose one of the three horns of the following trilemma: —

The words "we all," "each one of us," "every," must mean (1), all mankind, saints and sinners, or (2), the saints only, or (3), the wicked only. If either of the first two is chosen, the saints will be judged. But if the third is chosen, how do you account for the fact that St. Paul deliberately includes himself ("we" and "us") among the wicked? His constant habit is to use these pronouns either referring to all men, more commonly to believers. There is no instance of his classifying himself with unbelievers.

The same reasoning applies to 2 Cor. v. 10, with the addition of the fact that Paul here analyzes the words "we all" into two classes, those who have done good, and those who have done evil. This unanswerably demonstrates that the saints are not on the judgment seat as associate judges, but before that august tribunal. In Heb. ix. 27 — "It is appointed unto men once to die, but after this the judgment" — it is manifest that the judgment is co-extensive with death, and is in no way conditioned on character. Hence the saints will come into judgment after death. The strength of this argument is immediately perceived by the Greek scholar when he sees that the word for "men" is *anthropoi*, a term so broad as to comprehend the whole race. Then to make surety doubly sure, it is preceded by what grammarians call "the generic article," which must often be left untranslated in English, but means all the human race (Hadley, § 529).

We could hardly keep from laughing in the face of the venerable Christian scholar, when, at my request, Mr Darby gave an exposition of Matt. xxv. 31–46. What pitiable make-shifts to explain away this most solemn and awful passage in the Holy Scriptures! "It was not a final and universal judgment, but a review of the Gentile nations. Individuals are not here judged, but nations other than the Jews. The point to be determined is, how these nations have treated the Christianized Jews whom

Christ will send forth to convert the Gentiles after His coming and setting up of His visible kingdom on the earth. 'My brethren' are Jews. Jesus never called anybody brother but a Jew." But when pressed to explain more particularly the sheep and the goats, and the final sentence, the wriggling and floundering of this great evangelist was something wonderful to behold. May I never see another man, manifestly of so great genius and learning, compelled to crawl through orifices so small. There is something very depressing to a generous mind to witness such an intellectual humiliation in the attempt to save a baseless dogma from a manifest overthrow.

St. Paul, a thorough student of the Old Testament prophecies, and illumined by plenary inspiration, never interprets the Old Testament as predicting the literal return of the Jews. He spiritualizes the seed of Abraham, the sacrifices, the circumcision, and Jerusalem, and he distinctly foretells the spiritual salvation of the

Hebrews, not before "the fulness of the Gentiles be come in," but after that event (Rom. xi. 25). The faith of the Gentile world receiving Jesus as their Saviour will drown out the unbelief of the Jews, and they will receive Him as their Messiah. Is not this great Apostle, writing under the inspiration of the Holy Spirit, a more accurate interpreter of the prophets than any uninspired man, or class of men, in modern times?

The universal Church of Christ, from the beginning to the present hour, has never formulated pre-Millenarianism in its creed statements of Christian truth. They all speak of Christ as coming "to judge the quick and dead," but never to set up an outward and visible kingdom "with Jerusalem for the centre of worship and of blessing." Examine that summary of Christian faith, the Apostles' creed, so-called, not because it was made by them, but because it is a compend of their doctrines, and you will find no trace of Chiliasm contained therein. The judicious Bishop Pearson, in his Exposition of the Creed, says, "That the end for which He shall come, and the action which He shall perform when He cometh, is to judge all those which shall then be alive, and all which ever lived."

The Nicene Creed, better known and more generally recognized than any other, except the Apostles', teaches exactly the same doctrine with respect to the purpose of Christ's second advent, "to judge the quick and the dead." There is even a verbal agreement.

The next most important symbol of the early church, the Athanasian Creed, has these words: "Whence He shall come to judge the quick and dead. At whose coming all men shall rise again with their bodies, and shall give account of their works."

All these three great creeds agree in four points:—

1. That Christ will come again.
2. The object of His advent will be "to judge

the quick and the dead." This they testify with one voice, and as preliminary, all confess the resurrection of the dead, meaning all the dead.

3. All imply what the Athanasian distinctly states, that this resurrection and judgment will be at His coming.

4. All are silent about any pre-millennial coming, or personal reign, or any of the peculiar tenets of millenarians. Now these creeds universally received, in ancient and modern times, by Roman, Greek, and Protestant churches, must be presumed to accord with the Divine Word.

The Augsburg Confession, A. D. 1530, says: "It is taught that Christ will appear at the end of the world to sit in judgment, and that He will raise all the dead, and will give to the righteous and elect eternal life and endless joys; but wicked men and devils He will condemn, and they shall be tormented without end."

It adds this significant item: "Others are also condemned, who are now scattering Jewish notions, that prior to the resurrection the righteous will possess a temporal kingdom, and all the wicked will be exterminated."

Substantially the same clause, "to judge the quick and the dead," is found in the Metropolitan, 1530; Basle, 1534; Second Basle, 1536; Second Helvetic, 1564; Heidelburg, 1562; Belgic, 1562; Scotch, 1560; Anglican, 1551-1562; Westminster, 1643-48; Catechism of Trent, 1566; and Orthodox Confession, 1642.

This array of creeds, ancient and modern, Protestant, Papal, and Greek, teaches a doctrine wholly irreconcilable with the first principles of millenarianism, or modern Second Adventism. If it is true that all men are wiser than one man, it is true that all churches are more correct in a doctrine held in common than one small sect which sets up a doctrine inconsistent with it.

The prophecies adduced as teaching the

return of the Jews, and the temporal reign of Christ at Jerusalem, present a view of Christianity so grossly materialistic as to be absolutely irreconcilable with Christ's spiritual kingdom. Isaiah xiv. 1, 2, a commonly-quoted proof-text for the restoration of the Jews, declares that they will be slave-holders. "The house of Israel shall possess them (strangers) in the land of the Lord, for servants and handmaids." After the spirit of philanthropy, kindled in men's hearts by the Gospel, has led them to sweep every form of involuntary servitude from the earth, it is utterly repugnant to all our ideas of moral, not to say of Christian progress, to read that chattel slavery, the possession of slaves, will be re-established under the eye of Jesus, the visibly enthroned King. What a moral absurdity!

Again, Zech. xiv. 21, teaches that the returned Jews will offer animal sacrifices in Jerusalem, and boil the flesh in pots. How can this be reconciled with the abolition of the Levitical law, as taught by Paul? What would be the significance and efficacy of bloody sacrifices after the Lamb of God has been slain as a sufficient atonement for sin?

CHAPTER X.

THE PROPHETIC CONFERENCE REVIEWED.

CONSPECTUS OF ITS DOCTRINES.

The author has thought that he could give the best refutation of the Plymouth Eschatology by a republication of his review of "The Prophetic Conference," held in New York in 1878. It was published in *Zion's Herald*, soon afterward, in a series of eight articles.

The recent Prophetic Conference in New York, for the setting forth and advocacy of the general outline of the Plymouth scheme of last things, is the effect of causes which the writer has watched for several years with the deepest interest. It is the natural fruitage of the Plymouth literature brought from England and recommended to American Christians by certain popular evangelists in their sermons, Bible readings, and evangelical conferences. These evangelists, though they discard the name of

Plymouth Brethren, have sown broadcast their doctrines, with a zeal and earnestness rivaling the Brethren themselves.

The Conference was for the purpose of advocating the doctrine that the second coming of Christ is not, as is commonly believed, to raise the dead, judge the living and the dead, and wind up the history of the human race on the earth, but to raise the righteous dead, to set up a visible kingdom, and to reign in person on the earth during a thousand years. This is called *Chiliasm*, from the Greek, and *Millenarianism*, from the Latin, word for a thousand. But the more exact term is pre-millennialism — a term which describes the second advent as occurring before the thousand years. It may be interesting, before discussing its teachings, to look for a moment at the denominational complexion of the Prophetic Conference, which was composed of ministers and laymen, the former greatly preponderating; one Lutheran, one Dutch Reformed, one Reformed, ten Congregational, fifteen Episcopal, twenty-seven Baptist, forty-three Presbyterian, seven Methodist, and ten undenominational, which, we suppose, means Plymouth.

The first impression which this makes on the mind of a Methodist is that his Church has relatively the least stock in this concern. If we had been numerically represented, we would have had nearly a hundred. But this is not a matter which we are disposed to cry over. It indicates that Methodists are in too close a grapple with this present wicked world to sit down and waste time in speculating upon the future. It indicates that as a Church we are by no means so discouraged with the progress of the Gospel as to pronounce the dispensation of the Holy Spirit as inadequate to the conquest of the world for Christ. We shall see, as we review the strong Calvinism involved in the pre-millennial scheme, that there are theological reasons for the cold shoulder of Methodism. Eighty-one were from Calvinist and twenty-two from Arminian Churches. Of the papers on special topics read at the Conference, twelve were by Calvinists and three by Arminians.

It is not our purpose to go into a review of these papers in detail, but to outline the doctrines, and point out some difficulties in the way of our assent.

In nearly every paper and address there was a declaration that the world will never be conquered by the agencies now in the field; not because of any failure on the part of the Church to co-work with the Spirit, but because Christ never designed that the present dispensation should enthrone Him over the world. This is a merely preparatory dispensation to the future kingdom. The Church is not the kingdom, but a temporary institution for the training of a people whom Christ is taking out of the Gentiles for Himself. The kingdom cannot exist till the King is present in person, destroying pagan powers by force, and converting the people by the wholesale, by the majesty of His glorious presence. Yet this presence is to be localized at Jerusalem; the Jews are to rally around His uplifted standard, and to be converted immediately after His mounting the throne of David, and they, with all the zeal of young converts, are to go forth and preach Christ to the Gentiles with marvellous success. One of the speakers in the Conference assures us that everybody will then be converted. Just how free agency is adjusted to this statement the speaker did not tell us, though we are aching with a desire to know. But we suppose Dr. Imbrie would say that all are to be saved by irresistible grace. Hear him: "Regeneration is a glorious change in reference to this earth and the race upon it. It comprehends the appearing of the Saviour to accomplish it; the resurrection by Him of His departed saints, and the rapture (catching up) of His living saints to take part in His acts of dominion (holding offices under Him); *the overthrow of all forms of evil* on the earth; the repentance and restoration of Israel; the outpouring of the Spirit on all flesh; the renewal of the earth to far more than its original beauty before the curse; *the entire renewal of every child therein born*, and thus the atonement of Jesus made availing and applied to perpetual generations; the removal of all physical evils as well as *moral.*"

The parentheses and italics are ours. We cannot see why moral freedom in this scheme is not to be crushed out by almightiness, and converts to Christ are not to be made by sheer power, as the Pope converted tribes in northern Europe on the alternative of the sword or baptism. To our Arminian eye we see no difference. In the present dispensation men are converted by the suasion of the truth under the gentle and resistible influences of the Spirit. But in the future glorious regeneration of the earth, the Spirit, we are left to suppose, will drop the sword of the truth which failed before, and will come down upon the sinner with the trip-hammer of Omnipotence, crushing him into the die of sainthood in a twinkling.

But here comes the greatest wonder of all; why cannot a power, which irresistibly and infallibly converts, infallibly keep the soul in a gracious state? Dr. Imbrie insists that everybody will be converted in the millennium, or world's regeneration, but admits that when Satan is unchained, a countless host of these converts will so thoroughly backslide that Satan will deceive them into enlisting in a war against Christ in numbers " as the sand of the sea," going up on the breadth of the earth and compassing the camp of the saints about, and fire will come down from God out of heaven and devour them (Rev. xx. 7-9). So there will be a possibility of total apostasy under the glorious reign of the Person of King Jesus, while there is, according to Dr. Imbrie's Calvinism, no such possibility under the dispensation of the Holy Spirit. This is a wonder, indeed. But to us it is no surprise that machine-made Christians should fail when once the hand of almighty coercive power is removed from them. Converts made by force must be kept by force; those made by the suasion of truth may be kept by the same means, though Satan constantly roars along their path. Hence we believe that the present dispensation is the most favorable for the development and growth of virtue which this world will ever see, and that the future dispensation which exists in the dreams of Chiliasts — the personal reign of Christ in bodily form on the earth, cowing the wicked into subjection by the awe of His majestic and glorious presence — will not afford the conditions requisite to a fair probation. When free agency is overpowered by some motive of overwhelming weight, as in death-bed repentances, we are always on the lookout for spurious conversions. It is exceedingly difficult to make a virtuous choice under such a preponderance of terror. Hence we all exhort sinners not to defer submission to Christ till the hour of death.

Now, the second coming of Christ is always represented as a thousand-fold more awful than death. He will be revealed in flaming fire, with the holy angels, on the throne of His glory. If He sets up that throne, not as a judgment tribunal for the day of doom, but as a permanent government for a thousand years, He will have destroyed the very genius and spirit of the Gospel, which is the sway of human hearts by truth and love, and He will have inaugurated the reign of force instead. This will be stripping Christianity of its essential glory, the "grace and truth by Jesus Christ," and going back to the iron system of law which came by Moses. It will put the mount that quaked and burned with fire in the foreground, completely hiding Calvary from the sinner's eye. It will be a public confession that a fallen world cannot be restored by the moral power of truth and love under the suasion of the Paraclete, and a resort to force for the triumph of His kingdom.

We can see how an old-fashioned Calvinist, who believes in irresistible grace, can accept this doctrine; but how an Arminian, trained to magnify human freedom and the suasive power of Gospel motives for the renovation of the will, through the Holy Spirit applying truth assented to by the intellect, and taught to reject salvation by mere sovereignty, can accept the Millenarian idea of the universal triumph of Christ, surpasses our poor understanding.

But there is a greater wonder. If the world is to be subdued to Christ by a stroke of His omnipotence, and not by the slow process of redeeming love — the story of the Cross told o'er and o'er in ever-widening circles down the generations, till every creature has heard the glad evangel — why does not that stroke fall now, or, rather, why did it not fall thousands of years ago? If the world is growing worse and worse, and there is no hope for its salvation under the present Gospel agencies, it cannot be that the second coming of Christ to set up His kingdom is delayed through the Divine compassion and long-suffering; for these would prompt God to interpose immediately, or rather, it would have prompted Him to interpose long ago to prevent the race drifting hopelessly down to inevitable ruin. But if the coming of Christ is to institute the general judgment and execute the eternal doom of the incorrigible, and there is a remedial system gradually extending through all the earth, we have a good reason for the delay of Christ, the merciful Intercessor, to assume the office of an inexorable Judge. But if He foresees the inevitable failure of the gradual triumph of the Spirit, and if it is His purpose to discard this mode of saving men, and to disentangle Himself entirely from it, and to institute His kingdom by downright omnipotence, saving the race by force, why does He delay? The pre-millenarian can give no satisfactory answer.

CHAPTER XL.

DIFFICULTIES OF LITERALISM.

In our attempt to accept the teachings of this body of good men, we find an insuperable obstacle in their literal exegesis of Scriptures which are manifestly figurative. By way of illustration, we will examine their method of explaining Zech. xiv. In proof of the personal reign of Christ at Jerusalem, no Scripture is quoted more frequently and more confidently than portions of this chapter, especially the fourth and ninth verses: "And His (the Lord's) feet shall stand in that day upon the mount of Olives." "And the Lord shall be king over all the earth; in that day shall there be one Lord, and His name one." Now, we lay down as a canon of interpretation, that a homogeneous passage of God's Word must be expounded homogeneously; that is, it must be entirely literal or entirely symbolical. It will not do to mix these methods and dodge an absurd literalism by resorting to a figurative interpretation where the passage is a homogeneous unit. In the light of this principle let us go through this chapter, applying a literal exegesis.

In verse 2 "all nations" (not some, or all by representatives, but *all* the nations of the globe) "gather against Jerusalem to battle." This is, of course, to be as real and visible as Waterloo or Gettysburg, only a myriad-fold more bloody. Jesus Christ is to be in the field in bodily form as really as General Grant was in the battle of the Wilderness. Whether the Prince of Peace will "go forth" singly "and fight against those nations, as when He fought in the day of battle," or as a general in command of an army, is a question which is determined by the fifth and fourteenth verses, in which we find the Jewish brigade in the field and "all the saints" with the Lord.

The inference is, the saints will not stand as idle spectators, but will all have a hand in the fight. These saints are the righteous dead of all past ages, raised from their graves, and the living believers, who were all caught up to meet the Lord in the air, and who descended with Him at His appearing after receiving their reward — some office in the millennial kingdom. This scene brings vividly to mind the Homeric battles before the walls of Troy, where bloodless immortals — gods and demigods — sword in hand, mingled in the gory battles of the Greeks and Trojans. But a scrutiny of our Hebrew Bible develops another difficulty: "And Judah also shall fight *against* Jerusalem," not at Jerusalem. This complicates matters; for the Jews have all been converted, and have become Christ's foremost adherents. That they should turn against the capital city of their Messiah King, after He had gathered them to the land of their fathers, is something very mysterious. Will some Chiliast rise and explain?

But, in addition to all these difficulties, nature is to be convulsed, the mount of Olives to be cleft asunder, and a great valley to take its place, running eastward to the Dead Sea, through which a stream of water is to run, and another stream is to run westward to the Mediterranean, possibly, making a sea-port of Christ's capital. The convenience of this arrangement will be seen when we read that *every one* that is left of all the nations which come against Jerusalem, shall even go up, year by year, to worship the King, the Lord of hosts, and to keep the "feast of tabernacles." This going up of the whole world annually to Jerusalem, which, according to the Levitical law, must be done by families and not by proxy, would be quite impracticable for the Western nations, with the present difficult landing at Joppa, and a horse-back ride over the hills to the Holy City. How many ships it would take to carry, every year, the whole human family, or one half — say 700,000,000 — counting out the children, the very aged, and those near enough to Jerusalem to go by land, we leave to the pre-millennial arithmeticians. It would be safe to predict that the ocean-carrying business would be exceedingly lively, and that American shipping would not be so depressed as it has been since the great Rebellion.

In answer to the question how these annual pilgrims to the capital of the millennial kingdom are to be fed, and who is to carry on the world's agriculture, we have at hand the reply of Papias (A. D. 100), the first great millenarian: "In like manner a grain of wheat will produce ten thousand heads, and each head will bear ten thousand grains, and each grain will yield ten pounds of clear white flour; and other seeds will yield seeds and herbage in the same proportion." This fecundity of nature reduces the difficulty to that of a sufficient number of harvesters, millers and bakers. We infer from the statement of Irenæus that there may be some difficulty in securing the grape crop; "The days will come when vines shall grow, each bearing ten thousand branches, and on each branch there will be ten thousand twigs, and on each twig ten thousand clusters of grapes, and each grape, when expressed, will yield twenty-five *metratai* of wine (*i. e.*, about two hundred and nine gallons). And when any one of the saints shall take hold of a cluster, another cluster will cry out, 'I am a better cluster, take me, and on my account give thanks unto the Lord.'" We infer that when each grape-vine will produce wine to the amount of one hundred and eighty thousand billions of gallons, there will be plenty of work for Gough, Murphy, Dr. Reynolds and Frances E. Willard, during the thousand years of the good time coming; for even the saints may be in danger of repeating the folly, in their regenerated earth, that Noah did, in his renewed world, after all the sinners were drowned.

But let us return from this digression to our literal exposition. What are the human family to do after they have all been transported to Palestine? They are to keep the feast of tabernacles. They are to build booths in the streets of the city and on the house-tops. This will require considerable more space than Palestine itself can afford; for when people are on a joyous picnic it will not be in harmony with the spirit of the occasion to crowd them together like Africans in the hold of a slave-ship.

But this difficulty of literalism we must pass by, and inquire into the kind of religious service these pilgrims are expected to render. We find that in everything except circumcision they are commanded to be Jews. They must attend a localized worship as did the Jews; they must keep one of the great Jewish feasts, under pains and penalties for disobedience; "the Lord's house" will be standing, and there will be the "bowls"—literally, "sprinkling bowls" for blood-sprinkling, and the "pots" for seething the peace-offerings. In short, it is said that "they that sacrifice" shall come and take of them and seethe therein. "The altar" is spoken of, and its whole ritual is certainly implied as obligatory. The sacrificial slaughter of animals at the Lord's altar and in the Lord's house is spoken of undeniably. What will be the significance of these animal sacrifices after the one and sufficient sacrifice of the Lamb of God? Will some literalist who insists that Jesus will set up His throne at Jerusalem, be so kind as to tell us? It will not do to spiritualize the sacrifice unless you spiritualize the whole chapter.

Our explanation is very simple. When God would convey to the Jews the idea that in some future time all the human race would be worshippers of Him, he condescended to their own narrow notions of true worship, namely, coming to Jerusalem and offering sacrifice. The whole chapter is to be interpreted spiritually. The waters going eastward and westward symbolize a spiritual Christianity going forth from Jerusalem to refresh and save the world. The rending of the mountain to make way for the stream is the prophetic imagery in which is couched the prediction of the providential removal of obstacles in the way of the spread of the Gospel. Thus most of the difficulties of this obscure chapter vanish when we take a spiritual view.

Other difficulties press upon the literal interpretation of this chapter. We mention only one. If any people refuse to go up to Jerusalem, they are threatened with drought and the plague. Here both moral and natural evil, or suffering in consequence of sin, are treated as possibilities, in the very millennium. But, according to Dr. Imbrie, both natural and moral evil will be excluded. Who will relieve this discrepancy between millenarian teaching and the threatened punishments in this their favorite prophecy?

If any reader of Zech. xiv. still insists that the language must be literally interpreted, we advise him to read the eighteenth Psalm, in which David describes his deliverance from his enemies by divine interposition. Can the same reader believe that it is literally true of Jehovah — "There went up a smoke out of His nostrils, and fire out of His mouth devoured; coals were kindled by it," etc.? Then let the reader turn to Joel ii. 28–32, and read the graphic account which will convulse all nature, if understood literally. Then read Peter's exegesis of this Scripture as descriptive of the coming of the Paraclete (Acts ii. 17).

We venture to say that if Peter's exegesis were not on record, the modern pre-millennialists would stoutly assert that no event in past history corresponds to this picture of "the great and terrible day of the Lord;" and they would be applying the passage to some future upheaval of nature and miraculous revolution of society, whereas it related only to the coming and gentle sway of the Holy Spirit over believers and His work of convicting sinners.

CHAPTER XII.

PREDESTINARIAN BASIS.

We cannot receive the teachings of the Prophetic Conference by reason of its quite clearly-pronounced Calvinism. This is not a non-essential part of the scheme lugged in by the predestinarian essayists, but is fundamental in the system. The design of the dispensation of the Holy Spirit is not to save all men, but to take out of the Gentiles a people for Christ's name. These constitute His chosen Bride. He meets her for the first time in the air. She is to have special honors ever after. A large millennial family may spring from her, but they are inferior in dignity and privilege to the Bride, the Lamb's wife. Here we have an attempt to revive the moribund doctrine of unconditional election, by detaching and suppressing the twin tenet, unconditional reprobation.

Rev. Dr. A. J. Gordon, in his attempt to disprove the simultaneous resurrection of the human race at the second advent, and in his advocacy of the resurrection of the righteous, as "special and eclectic," a thousand years before the rising of the wicked, speaks thus: "The doctrine of election, which we profess to hold, should not be a mere abstraction of theology, an article of faith which we find it necessary to adopt in order to insure a consistent and Scriptural body of divinity, while we ignore its practical application. It is, perhaps, the most solemn and awful of all Scriptural revelations. It certainly can only be discussed and preached effectively by us in those rare states of mind where the exquisite balance has been reached between tender adoration of the sovereignty and holiness of God, and pathetic sympathy with the helplessness and sinfulness of man. While, therefore, it is the instinct of the truest piety to leave God to carry out what belongs wholly to the domain of His will, it should be equally the care of an exact and loyal theology to note the application of this principle at the various stages of redemption, and speak accordingly. Thus we speak very constantly of our missionary enterprises as destined to convert the heathen nations to Christ. The Holy Spirit says that God has visited the Gentiles, 'to take out of them a people for His name.' We speak about the world being converted. The Lord said to His first disciples what He says to us, and what He will say, we believe, to the last that shall be converted under this dispensation: 'Ye are not of this world, but I have chosen you out of the world.' We speak of Christ's coming at the last day to a race that has been redeemed and saved under the preaching of the Gospel. Christ, in speaking of that event, says that 'the Son of Man will send His angels to gather together his elect,' etc. We speak of all men being raised up together at the appearance of the Lord to be judged. Christ speaks of those who shall be 'accounted worthy to obtain that age and the resurrection from among the dead.'"

In this long quotation the reader will note a quiet rebuke for what "we say," in the use of terms which indicate the universality of the divine regards, and of the redemptive plan, and he will observe a narrowing of it down to the elect, the selection of whom " belongs *wholly* to the domain of God's will." Thus it seems that we modern Christians, theologians and missionary boards, have become broader in our views and aims than our great Founder, Christ Himself. To be sure, He once said something about preaching His gospel to every creature, but He intended that it should be only a common call to all, while the Holy Spirit, who had looked into the depths of the Father's secret will, and had seen the names of the elect — a definite number — written there, would infallibly give these a special call, accompanied by irresistible grace. Hence it was absolutely certain before the foundation of the world that every person whose name was on that precious register, hidden in the bosom of God, would be found arrayed in white at the descent of His Son, the Bridegroom.

Dr. Gordon's resurrection for the elect only, needs only an atonement for the elect alone to put a very handsome finish upon the system, making it symmetrical and beautiful. This lacking ornament is supplied by Rev. H. M. Parsons, in his paper on "The Present Age and the Development of Anti-Christ." Hear him: "Each age (religious dispensation) had its assigned work in the recovery of heaven. Our own age has its section. It is to gather from out the nations (Gentiles) the redeemed people of God." Here is plainly taught the doctrine that the Gentiles are not redeemed, but only a people scattered among them are redeemed. The old doctrine of a limited atonement, preached in New England a century ago, but now almost universally banished by the presence of a biblical Arminianism, creeps forth again into the light of day in this convention of the prophets. Hear the peroration of Mr. Parsons: " Brethren and friends, we are called to preach the Gospel to every creature during this age, that from every nation, and tongue, and people, the Lord Jesus may gather in His dear Bride." We have always supposed that our commission was to every creature because Jesus Christ tasted death for every man. But according to Calvinian Millenarianism, we are to preach to every creature only because Christ omitted to put a chalk-mark on His Bride. If this mark had been made, it would have simplified our work, and we could pass by those whom Christ did not intend to woo and to wed, and devote all our efforts to the affianced ones, on whom He has set His heart. What a pity that preachers should be required to waste so much labor!

Many things in the paper of Dr. James H. Brooks were to us a means of grace, especially his vigorous and exhaustive presentation of the bearing of the coming of Christ on the fidelity and purity of believers. But we found no nutriment to our spiritual life when we read the following sentence: "The pre-millennial coming of our Lord alone indicates the divine honor and *sovereignty*. Those who reject the doctrine, constantly affirm that it disparages the Gospel by representing it as a failure, and the work of the Holy Spirit, by intimating that it is inadequate to the conversion of the world. But a moment's reflection is sufficient to show that it exalts the Gospel by proving that *it accomplishes all it was designed to effect*, and the work of the Holy Spirit by demonstrating that *He saves all He intended to save during the present dispensation*." If the words we have italicized "exalt the Gospel," they certainly blacken the character of its Author with a heartless indifference to the well-being of a portion of our race while pretending a deep interest in their salvation, and in mockery offering them everlasting life which they could not appropriate without the assistance of the Spirit. Whittier tells us that the indignant women of Marblehead "tarred and feathered the sea captain, Floyd Ireson, and rode him on a cart" for not saving some poor fellows on a raft at sea when he saw their signals of distress. That he did not *intend* to save them was his crime against humanity, which outraged the moral sense and philanthropic instincts of these plucky women. It would have made the case no better, but rather worse, if that seaman had changed his course, gone to the wreck, taken off all that he *intended* to, and then sailed away, with abundant room in his cabin and provisions in his larder for those whom he had left to perish on the raft.

It would certainly be an alleviation of Dr. Brooks' doctrine, to attach to it the grand scheme of restorationism advocated by Mr. Barbour, of Rochester, by which all those whom the Holy Spirit did not *intend* to save under the present dispensation, will be raised from the dead and have a fair chance for salvation in the millennial age. The only difficulty in this theodicy is the fact that the wicked dead must remain in their graves, and not be raised till after the millennium is past, when they will be raised, judged, and cast into the lake of fire. So our suggested alleviation is an adjustment which cannot be applied.

A class of millenarians, not represented in the report of the Prophetic Conference, have found out just the number that the Holy Spirit intends to save and to present to Christ as His bride — 144,000. By scrupulously keeping the seventh day, and abstaining from meats ceremonially unclean, they are endeavoring to be among that number. They are the dolefulest saints we ever met. We think they should be despondent, with such a slender hope of salvation.

CHAPTER XIII.

EXEGETICAL ABSURDITIES.

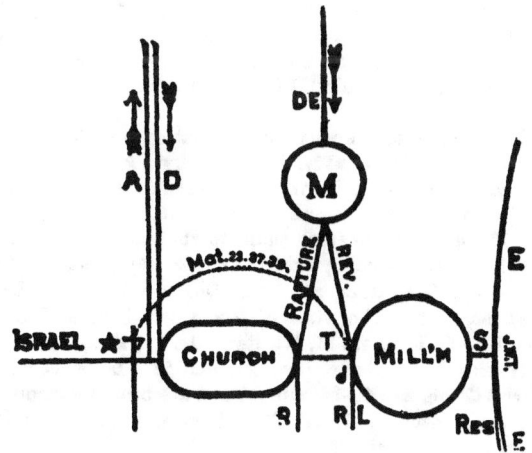

* — The birth of Christ, the King of the Jews. Matt. ii. 2.
† — The death and resurrection of Christ.
A — Ascension of Christ. Acts i. 9.
D — Descent of the Holy Ghost. Acts ii.

ANTINOMIANISM REVIVED.

Church—Mystical body of Christ (Eph. i. 22, 23; iii. 3–6; Rom. xii. 4, 5; Col. i. 24–27; 1 Cor. xii. 12–27,) and the Bride of Christ. Eph. v. 21–23.

De—Descent of the Lord (1 Thess. iv. 14) to receive His Bride. John xiv. 3.

R—Resurrection of the just. Luke xiv. 14; Acts xxiv. 15; 1 Thess. iv. 15, 16; and change of living believers. 1 Cor. xv. 23, 51, 52.

Rapture—Translation of the saints who (like Enoch) are caught up to meet Christ in the air. 1 Thess. iv. 17.

M—The meeting of Christ and His Bride. 1 Thess. iv. 17; Eph. v. 21–32; 2 Cor. xi. 2. Thus the Church escapes the tribulation. Luke xxi. 36; 2 Peter ii. 9; Rev. iii. 10.

T—Period of unequalled tribulation to the world (Dan. xii. 1; Matt. xxiv. 21; Luke xxi. 25, 26) during which—the Church having been taken out—God begins to deal with Israel again (Acts xv. 16, 17; Psa. li. 18; cii. 16,) and will restore them to their own land. Isa. xi. 11–16; Jer. xxx. 3; xxxi; xxxii. 36–44; Amos ix. 15; Zech. viii. 3–8; Rom. xi. Anti-Christ will be revealed. 2 Thess. ii. 8. The vials of God's wrath poured out. Psa. ii. 1–5; Rev. vi. 16, 17; Rev. xiv. 10; xvi. But men only blaspheme God. Rev. xvi. 11, 21. Israel accepts Christ (Zech. xii. 10–14; xiii. 6,) and are brought through the fire. Zech. xiii. 9. They pass not away. Matt. xxiv. 34; Psa. xxii. 30.

Rev—The revelation of Christ and His saints (Col. iii. 4; 1 Thess iii. 13) in flaming fire (2 Thess. i. 7–10) to execute judgment on the earth. Jude 14, 15. This is Christ's second coming to the earth. Acts i. 11; Deut. xxxiii. 2; Zech xiv. 4, 5; Matt. xvi. 27; xxiv. 29, 30.

J—Judgment of the nations, or the quick. Matt. xxv.

32-46; xix. 28; Acts x. 42; 1 Peter iv. 5. Anti-Christ is destroyed. 2 Thess. ii. 8. The Beast and the False Prophet are taken. Rev. xix. 20. Gog and His allies are smitten. Ezek. xxxviii.; xxxix. Satan is bound. Rev. xx. 1-3; Rom. xvi. 20.

R. L.— Resurrection of the Tribulation Saints, which completes the First Resurrection. Rev. xx. 4-6.

Mill'm — The Millennium. Christ's glorious reign on earth for 1,000 years (Rev. xx. 4) with His bride. 2 Tim. ii. 12; Rev. v. 10; Isa. ii. 2-5; iv.; xi. 1-12; xxv. 6-9; Isa. lxv. 18-25; Mic. iv. 1-4; Zeph. iii. 14-20; Zech. viii. 3-8, 20-23; xiv. 16-21.

S — Satan loosed for a little season, and destroyed with Gog and Magog. Rev. xx. 7-10; Heb. ii. 14.

Res.— The Resurrection of Judgment. Rev. xx. 12-15; John v. 29; Dan. xii. 2.

J. W. T.— Judgment at the Great White Throne of all the remaining dead. Rev. xx. 11-15. Death and Hell destroyed, Rev. xx. 14; 1 Cor. xv. 26.

E. E.— Eternity. Isa. lvii. 15.

[THE above diagram is taken from a pamphlet circulated at the Conference with the endorsement of its president. It is also found in a book entitled " Maranatha," by Rev. J. H. Brooks, one of the speakers in the Conference, and the first signer of the call. It is the basis of most of the papers as reported in the *Tribune.*]

The most vulnerable point of this pre-millenarian theory is found in the exegesis of Matt. xxv. 31–46. The necessities of the theory require its advocates to do violence to this most solemn utterance of the Son of God while on the earth. It is indisputable that He discloses four facts in this passage: (1) The judgment will be general, including the whole human race. (2) The righteous and the wicked will be simultaneously judged and sentenced. (3) The judgment will be individual, and not national; each person will be rewarded or condemned according to his treatment of Jesus Christ in the persons of His brethren, either believers or human beings generally. (4) This day of judgment is a finality, a winding-up of the history of man on the earth. Henceforth mankind will be found in only two conditions — in everlasting punishment or in life eternal — with the intimation that the former is a *place* prepared for the devil and his angels. The pre-millenarian, finding it impossible to wedge in an earthly reign of Christ, called the millennium, between the coming of the Son of Man in His Glory and His final sentence, "Come, ye blessed!" and "Depart, ye cursed!" deliberately goes to work to pervert these awful words by whittling them down to a review of living nations, ending in the infliction of certain temporal punishments which do not sweep them from the earth, but leave them still living, to be converted or held in check, by millennial agencies.

This is the teaching of the Prophetic Conference. We call this the willful perversion of the plain words of Jesus Christ, the Judge eternal. If the reader will look at the above diagram, he will find the letter J descriptive of the place which the judgment in Matt. xxv. 31–46, occupies in the Chiliast's eschatology. Instead of being the end of man on the earth, it is about the middle point of his earthly history, and he will be found, after the sentence of eternal doom, begetting children (Isa. xi. 6, 8; lxv. 23), black-smithing (Isa. ii. 4), house-building and vine-planting (Isa. lxv. 21), the old man with his staff in hand for very age, and the boys and girls playing in the streets (Zech. viii. 4, 5); while others shall suffer from plagues inflicted on them and their cattle, and still others will go to battle and gather great spoil (Zech. xiv. 13–15). The references are those which accompany the diagram.

One of the essayists, Dr. J. T. Cooper, argued that only the Gentiles are judged in Matt. xxv. 31–46, and that the Jews were exempt. According to this writer, and the Plymouth teachers generally, this judgment turns upon the question how each nation has treated Christ's brethren, the Jews. Let the reader peruse this whole passage, putting *nations*, or *Gentiles*, after the pronouns "ye" and "you," and in place of "them," and substitute *Jews* for "my brethren," and he will get some idea of the monstrous misinterpretation which Chiliasm is forced to put upon this plain passage, in defiance of common sense.

By making two *last* (?) days, or judgment days — one for the living and one for the dead (Rev. xx. 11-15) — a space is gained for the millennium after the Second Advent. It is nothing to these expositors that the words, the "quick" and the "dead," in Acts x. 42; 2 Tim. iv. 1; 1 Peter iv. 5, are thus violently riven asunder by thrusting in a thousand years between them. Jesus says: "For the hour is coming in the which *all* that are in their graves shall hear His voice, and shall come forth; they that have done good unto the resurrection of life, and they that have done evil unto the resurrection of damnation." Here Dr. Gordon finds no difficulty, by stretching "the hour," to make two resurrections, a thousand years apart! The millenarians find no difficulty in splitting the judgment day into fragments, locating one in the air before the Epiphany, or appearing of Christ, another on the earth after that event, and still another after a thousand years. The Plymouth Brethren add a fourth judgment day, when the sins of believers were judged on the Cross — the only judgment of their persons as distinguished from their works. But since the resurrection is always intimately connected with the judgment, this theory easily invents as many resurrections as are requisite to its demands. Hence we have a resurrection of the saints, to meet Christ before He descends to the earth; then the resurrection of the martyrs, who by some unaccountable agency have been converted and beheaded while Christ was reviewing the saints in the air, and not a holy soul was left on the earth, but Antichrist was for years, and perhaps centuries, riding roughshod over the God-forsaken earth, and all the woes and vials of the Apocalypse were being poured upon the human race, amid the crash of all the regular governments and the horrors of anarchy. Then we have a third resurrection — that of the wicked — after a thousand years *plus* the period in which Satan is loosed, which may be ten thousand years more. For all these resurrections and judgments Scripture proofs are quoted with great profusion and perfect confidence, although the Church from the beginning till the present day has believed in one resurrection and one judgment of the whole human family.

But still greater difficulties, not to say absurdities, are encountered when we examine the mixed state of things on the earth after the judgment of the living nations, or "the quick." Here we find living side by side in the millennium the remnant who have survived the judgment, and are still flesh and blood; the saints who were changed when the Judge reached the air; and the righteous dead who have been raised and endowed with spiritual bodies. How these three sorts of folks are to have intercourse — mortals and immortals thus mixed together — is inconceivable. But as children are to be born, still more difficult social problems arise. There will be a class capable of marriage, because they are still in the flesh; a class incapable of that estate, because they are "in the resurrection;" and a class of whom we are doubtful, namely, the changed saints. This exceeding complex state of society is entirely out of analogy with the constitution and course of nature, and is entirely abnormal and incongruous.

The moral government of such a world by the second Person of the Trinity in person will be one continued reign of supernaturalism, wholly unadapted to the purposes of probation. The change will be so great that there will be need of a new Bible, for the new state of things will render the Holy Scriptures as obsolete as Noah's almanac. This is admitted by distinguished pre-millenarians. One of them is quoted by Bickersteth as saying that "the Scriptures of the New Testament, written for a tempted and suffering Church, are unapplicable to this state of things." Dr. McNeile says: "It is obvious that, in the passage from our present state to a state of universal holiness, these characteristic sayings of the New Testament must cease to have any application, and become obsolete, not to say false."

If the human race is to be continually propagated through a thousand, or, as some assert, through three hundred and sixty-five thousand years, and none die, the world would soon be so uncomfortably crowded that there would not be standing room. But if death does his work of depletion then as now, only after a longer average longevity — the child dying an hundred years old — there must be another resurrection distinct from that of the wicked for the accommodation of these deceased millennial saints. This will make four resurrections in all. Thus the difficulties thicken as we dwell on this theory of the personal reign of Christ on earth before the last day, which is certainly "another gospel" from that which Paul preached.

To the people of the United States this judgment of nations by the test of our national treatment of the Jews, is one which we may approach with greater boldness than any other nation of modern civilization, for we have never discriminated against the Hebrews, " these my brethren," in our legislation, though we have abused the African, the Indian, and the Chinaman, who are not supposed to be so closely related to Jesus Christ. Hence the great American Republic stands a good chance to be the dominant nation in the regeneration, or millennial age, which begins immediately after the award to the nations of eternal life or everlasting punishment.

CHAPTER XIV.

DIFFICULTIES IN THE THOUSAND YEARS.

WE object to the millenarian scheme, because it is grounded chiefly on those portions of the Bible which are symbolic, and enigmatic, and difficult to be understood. The personal reign of Christ a thousand years is not found in the Gospels, nor in the Acts of the Apostles, nor in the Epistles of Paul, Peter, James or John, but only in the Apocalypse, which is the darkest book in the New Testament. Its striking symbols and gorgeous imagery impress the imagination and awaken the feelings. The visitor in London will find in one library a thousand commentaries on this book, all professing to unfold its mysteries, all differing, so that only one of them can be true. These writers have tried to interpret the apocalyptic numbers, and they have signally failed. From

Bengel's date of the binding of Satan in 1836 down to the present time, the years fixed for the coming of Christ have passed away, and the expositors who have survived their disappointment have courageously tried again, by shifting their ground into the safer future. There are three great schools of interpreters of the Revelation: (1) The Præterists, or those who teach that the whole, or by far the greater part, has been fulfiled. Some of the most eminent German expositors, as Ewald, De Wette, Lucke, and Dusterdieck, belong to this school; also Dr. Davidson in England, and Moses Stuart in America. (2) The Historicals, who hold that the Revelation embraces the whole history of the Church to the end of the world. (3) The Futurists, who insist that this book, after the third chapter, relates entirely to future events. Some include the first three chapters, and assert that they refer to the future also.

This is the grand outline of opinions held by

men equally learned and honest; yet on a book whose interpretation is in so great dispute, the doctrine of a thousand years' personal reign of Christ on the earth before the last judgment is grounded by those who would interpret the plain and the literal teachings respecting the last things by the symbolic and typical, thus inverting an acknowledged canon of interpretation. The twentieth chapter of the Revelation is the basis of pre-millenarianism. Let us now examine this chapter, and see what is not proved by its testimony.

1. There is no mention of the second advent of Christ before the thousand years. The chapter opens with the vision of an angel descending from heaven with a chain in his hand. This angel can never be proved to be Christ. Says Alford: "*Angelos*, in this book, is an *angel; never our Lord.*" Thus far in the Apocalypse there is not the slightest intimation that He has made His second advent in visible form. In chapter xix. 11–21, He wars against

the beast, and the kings of the earth and their armies; but the assumption that this is a literal battle fought on the earth by Jesus in person, riding on a white horse, with a sharp sword going out of His mouth, is a literalism which cannot be endured, besides being a begging of the very question in dispute. John saw the things in the opened heaven, and he saw "the armies which were in heaven." The Scriptures are unanimous in making heaven the fixed abode of Christ, until He shall come to judge mankind at the last day.

2. John saw only the *souls* of the martyrs. He makes no mention of their bodies. There is a grave doubt whether a bodily resurrection is here intended; but we are inclined to the literal resurrection of these martyrs. In John v. 25, we have a resurrection of souls, followed in verse 28 by a bodily resurrection. This, in the opinion of many, explains the first and the second resurrections in this chapter. The passage is obscure, admitting of different interpretations.

8. There is here no proof of the resurrection of all the righteous dead, but only of the beheaded martyrs; so that allowing the literal resurrection of these does not prove that all the saints rise at this time. Every man is to rise in his own order. Some arose at the resurrection of Christ, and doubtless were His convoy to heaven. It may be that a special honor and blessedness await the beheaded martyrs in the fact of their resurrection and translation to heaven before the rest of the dead saints: "for one star differeth from another star in glory." This does not preclude these from standing with Enoch and Elijah, in holy boldness, before the judgment seat of Christ in the last day. This may explain Paul's aim at a martyr's death and the resurrection of the beheaded (Phil. iii. 10, 11). "On such the second death hath no power." The dying of these martyrs, in a manner so heroic, utterly vanquished the mighty enemy. An early restoration from the dominion of death, suffered prematurely for

Christ, is an eminently appropriate reward: "Holy and blessed is he that hath part in the first resurrection."

4. There is in this chapter a total absence of proof that these raised martyrs reigned with Christ *on the earth*. The visions thus far have been located in heaven. Consistency with the whole context requires that they should reign *with Christ* in heaven, and not that Christ should reign with them on earth. Bengel, Wesley, Moses Stuart, and many others, say, "in heaven and not on the earth."

5. There is no evidence here that a single millennium is spoken of. The best scholars, and among them Bengel, Wesley, and Dr. Owen, assert that there are two distinct periods of a thousand years spoken of in verses 1–7. The Greek article sustains this view. The first period extends through the repression of Satan which, Bengel says, indicates the great prosperity of the Church. The second is the reign of martyrs. Both of these periods are before

the second coming of Christ. Thus Bengel and Wesley, instead of being pre-millenarians, were, in fact, what most modern Methodists are, post-millenarians. Bengel styles those who confound these two distinct millennial periods, "pseudo-Chiliasts." The Prophetic Conference thus falls under Bengel's censure as *pseudos*. He says: "Whilst Satan is loosed from his imprisonment of a thousand years, the martyrs live and reign, not on the earth, but with Christ; *then* the coming of Christ in glory at length takes place at the last day; *then*, next, there is the new heaven, the new earth, and the new Jerusalem." Thus the coming of Christ is two thousand years *plus* a little season after the binding of Satan. A harmless sort of Chiliasm is this. Says Bengel: "The confounding of the two millennial periods has long ago produced many errors, and has made the name of Chiliasm hateful and suspected."

6. It is a very important point for the millenarian to prove, that the judgment of the

dead before the great white Throne is that of the wicked dead only. But this vital point is not proven by this chapter. In fact, the bringing forth of the Book of Life and the casting into the lake of fire of those whose names are not written therein, imply that some were found inscribed. Dr. Brooks' declaration that this Book of Life is a blank book, is a baseless assumption. This is not proved by the words, "the rest of the dead lived not," etc. Says so eminent a Greek scholar as Dr. Owen: "Yet as the words here stand, we cannot, without great violence, make 'the rest' (in Greek) embrace any other than the class of the pious dead, from which the martyr saints have been previously taken to participate in the first resurrection." We quote Dr. Owen, not to endorse him, but to show the difficulty of proving that this is a judgment of the wicked dead alone.

We believe that it is the general judgment of the race described in Matt. xxv. 31–46, and that "the rest of the dead" include all the human dead, both righteous and wicked, except the martyr saints, and that the good and the bad will be raised in the general resurrection and sentenced in the general judgment.

7. We look in vain, in this account of the millennium, or millenniums, for any reference to the Jews as being gathered to Jerusalem. The Revelation strangely omits to associate them with either of these chiliads. In chapter seven, the angels seal exactly twelve thousand of each of the twelve tribes, but there is no hint of the restoration of the Hebrew nation to their own land. After the day of general doom, the last great day, there descends a new Jerusalem into the new earth which has no more sea. Even then "the tabernacle of God is with men," not with the Jews.

Considering the fact that the old Testament prophecies are constantly quoted by the millenarians in proof of the personal reign of Christ on earth, with the Jews as His most loyal supporters, it is to us an insuperable objection to the doctrine, that the book of Revelation omits to place the restored Hebrew nation in any such relation to Christ, either in the old or the new Jerusalem.

If there is to be a personal reign of Christ on the earth, during a thousand years, to subdue the nations, as a substitute for the conquest now being made by the Holy Spirit, it is remarkable that these seven essential facts should be absent from the only account in the whole Bible where the millennial period is spoken of.

These important items are culled from dark prophecies, often violently wrenched from the context, and are fitted together on the pedestal of this chapter of a book which has been an inexplicable enigma to the scholarship of all the Christian ages. This style of interpretation may be satisfactory and convincing to those who accept imagery for doctrine, symbol for substance, and rhetoric for logic; but there are Christian minds which have an unconquerable aversion to stitching together selections from the symbolry of the prophets, literalizing the whole patchwork, and holding it up to the world as God's truth. Yet this is what the pre-millenarians are perpetually doing. They opened their recent Conference with the disclaimer that they had not brought their ascension robes with them. But such is the perilous fascination of their method of prophetic studies, that they will soon be attracted to an interpretation of the apocalyptic numbers and a determination of the year and day when, in the language of Mr. Barbour, "Christ is due," as we say of an express train. History always repeats itself. This has been the outcome of every great millenarian movement. The leaders may keep their own intellectual balance quite well, but by deluging Christendom with their literature, they will soon shake the minds of Christians of less steadiness who will insist on bringing to the next Prophetic Conference their arithmetical charts of Daniel's animals, if not their ascension robes. We who survived 1843 know the sequel.

CHAPTER XV.

THE CHURCH NOT THE KINGDOM.

WE object to the pre-millenarian theory because its definition of the kingdom of Christ makes it an institution altogether different from the Church, and entirely in the future. A glance at the diagram will show the church as coming to an end on the earth before the kingdom is set up. The Chiliast represents the kingdom as coming only at the descent of the King in person, and as then set up suddenly by almightiness without the aid of human agency. But when we look into the New Testament, we find no such difference in the use of the terms "Church" and "kingdom." They seem to be used interchangeably. The kingdom is to be established by preaching, and it is to develop gradually till its ultimate triumph. The generation to whom John the Baptist and Christ preached, were urged to repent because the kingdom of heaven was at hand. We fail to see the cogency of this motive if the kingdom was not to be set up till after 1,800 or 18,000 years. St. Paul writes a thanksgiving epistle to the Colossians in which he expresses his gratitude to the Father "who hath translated us into the kingdom of His dear Son." Christ himself spoke of the kingdom of God as within, or among, His hearers. The disciples were taught to pray for its complete triumph on the earth. Parables illustrative of its slow progress, but ultimate universality, were spoken. The kingdom of heaven is like a grain of mustard-seed, which becomes a tree so great that the birds lodge in the branches. The astonishing development of Christ's kingdom from small beginnings through long ages is here plainly taught. It is perfectly puerile to assume that these birds are foul birds of prey, symbolizing the gigantic corruptions of the Christian Church! Yet we have again and again met with this exegesis in the writings of modern millenarians.

In Christ's comparison of the kingdom to leaven deposited in the meal, He intended to teach the gradual diffusion, the pervasive and assimilative power, and the universal prevalence of the kingdom of heaven. Every unprejudiced reader, even in the infant Sunday-school, sees this meaning in the parable. How do the Chiliasts dispose of this parable? The wise ones do as the Scotch preacher did with a passage which he could not harmonize with predestination: "My brethren, let us look this verse square in the face and pass on." But some millenarians are not wise enough to follow so good an example, but confidently expound it thus: "Leaven is always used in the Bible to represent evil or corruption." Hence in the language of Rev. H. M. Parsons: "The parable of the leaven represents the results which will be manifested in the same kingdom during the age from the corruptions introduced by those who are within the Church. The meal will be leavened with heresies and perversions during all this dispensation."

Well may Dean Alford say: "It will be seen that such an interpretation cannot for a moment stand, on its *own* ground; but much less when we connect it with the parable of the mustard-seed. The two are intimately related. The latter was of the *inherent, self-developing power* of the kingdom of heaven as a seed containing in itself the principle of expansion; the former (the leaven) represents *the power which it possesses of penetrating and assimilating a foreign mass,* till all be taken up into it. This gifted annotator, a strong Chiliast, but not run mad with millenarian vagaries, proceeds at length to show the power of the Gospel leaven (1) to penetrate the *whole mass of humanity,* and (2) the transforming power of the "new leaven" on the *whole being of individuals.* Says Trench: "In fact, the parable does nothing less than set forth to us the mystery of regeneration, both in its first act, which can be but once, as the leaven is but once hidden; and also in the consequent renewal of the Holy Spirit, which, as the ulterior working of the leaven, is continual and progressive." Thus we array these scholarly and sober expositors against the strange and erroneous exegesis of millenarians so intent on removing a difficult text out of their way that they foist upon it a meaning never intended by Christ, in order to make Him teach their doleful doctrine, that the church is becoming more and more corrupt, the world is hopelessly shipwrecked, and the pentecostal dispensation is a stupendous failure. From such a dismal view of Christianity, and from such a misinterpretation of a plain parable, giving a hopeful view of the expansion and universal prevalence of the kingdom of heaven established by Christ, we beg to be delivered.

We believe with Neander that the relation of the Church to the kingdom is that of a species to a genus, or of a part to a whole. The Church is the kingdom begun.

The millenarian conception of the earthly kingdom of Christ, entirely different from His present spiritual reign in the Church, is strikingly like the Jewish idea of the Messianic kingdom, founded on a literal interpretation of the prophecies. If their gross literalism is at last to be realized in an earthly and visible kingdom, we do not see the culpability of the Jews in rejecting the Nazarene, who failed to exhibit those signs of Messiahship which their own prophets had taught them to expect when His kingdom should be set up. For it has been well said that there is no perspective in prophecy. Hence it was absolutely impossible for the Jews to discriminate between Christ's first coming to found His Church, and His second advent to found His kingdom. The brightness of the earthly kingdom so entirely eclipsed the colorless, spiritual kingdom, or Church, that the Hebrew nation seems to be justified in discarding the spiritual kingship of Jesus Christ, who was attended by no such signs of worldwide temporal dominion as the millenarians now find in the Old Testament prophecies. But there is no such vindication of the Jews possible, because their culpability lies in the fact that while there is but one kingdom of Christ on earth, and that is spiritual, they were, as a nation, not dwelling in those spiritual altitudes which would have enabled them to view the Star of Bethlehem in its true character, undimmed by the clouds of sensuality and worldliness. Hence, on the commonly-received view that the Church is the spiritual kingdom of Christ, and the only kingdom which He will establish on earth, the ancient and modern Jews have no excuse. On the theory of the Chiliast, they have an excuse for rejecting Him who came to them without the prophetic insignia of a king.

No Motive for a Jew to Believe in Christ.

Another very curious fact in the millenarian scheme is that the nearer the Second Advent, the less influential is it to induce in the Jew submission to Christ. Let me amplify this point: My commission is to preach the Gospel to every creature. This includes the Jews. Let me suppose that I have a congregation of Hebrews whom I wish to lead to Christ. My first effort would be to gain an intellectual assent to the proposition that Jesus is the true Messiah, by reasoning with them in Pauline style out of the Scriptures. Having produced an intellectual conviction, I should next proceed to sway their wills to an immediate acceptance of the Nazarene as their personal Saviour. What would be my great argument? "The Lord Jesus shall be revealed from heaven, with His mighty angels, in flaming fire, taking vengeance on them that know not God and that obey not the Gospel of our Lord Jesus Christ, who shall be punished with everlasting destruction from the presence of the Lord and from the glory of His power." My Israelites, in terror, ask me if this is a final and irreversible sentence for disobedience to Christ. I tell them, with tears, that it is even so. Under the power of the Spirit attending the Word, some are constrained to bow the knee to Christ crucified who had been a stumbling-block to them all their lives. Knowing the terrors of the Lord, I have saved some. But suppose I had called in a millenarian to do this critical work of presenting motives to sway their stubborn Jewish wills? His course of argument would be thus: Repent of your sins, and receive Jesus as your Saviour and Lord because He is soon coming to set up a kingdom, gathering the Jews, at least a third of them, to Jerusalem, where they will all be suddenly converted and be the chief promoters of His kingdom among the Gentiles. "How long," ask they, "before this great event?" "It may occur to-day; all the signs indicate that it is near," is the answer. "If this is so, we think that we will not put ourselves to the inconvenience and suffering of the persecution of our brethren for embracing

Jesus. We will wait and take our chances of being alive and of being converted *en masse* when Jesus comes. This will be easier, and will be attended by no persecution by a stubborn remainder." Thus the nearer the Second Advent, the less is its motive power for the Jew to believe in Christ.

Can such a system of doctrine be true which thus weakens the grand motive to evangelical faith? The common, or orthodox, view of the second coming of Christ to pass final sentence upon the race, affords just as great inducements to repent to the Jew as to the Gentile, and the motive in both cases is intensified by the near approach of the Judge eternal.

CHAPTER XVI.

ELECT NUMBER OF THE GENTILES.

Having shown that the personal reign of Christ for a thousand years before the general judgment is not found in Rev. xx., we proceed to examine other passages in the New Testament perpetually quoted as proofs of Chiliasm. Matt. xix. 28 is literally expounded by Chiliasts, and the "regeneration" is explained as the new order of things on the earth after Christ has set up a visible throne. Then the twelve apostles are to have inferior thrones, or governorships, over the twelve tribes of Israel. In answer to this we cannot do better than to condense the comment of Dr. Whedon, one of the ripest Greek scholars in America, and second to none as an exegete: The words "in the regeneration" are in contrast with "in my temptations" in the parallel passage in Luke xxii.

28–30. The contrasted periods are before His death and after His ascension, when the Church was renewed and regenerated from the old to the new dispensation. Then Jesus would sit on the throne of his glory at the right hand of the Majesty on high till He shall, on the same throne, descend to judge the world. The twelve apostles were to receive twelve apostolates, or thrones — not thrones of glory — symbolizing the fact that Christ is King over Israel, and that the New Testament kingdom is only another form of the Old Testament Church. Then follows, in verse 29, a promise of the hundred-fold now in this time (Mark x. 30), with persecutions, showing that the time spoken of when the twelve should enjoy their apostolates, or sit on their spiritual thrones, is during their present lives, after which they will receive life everlasting. Hence we are living in the regeneration, or new dispensation. Another text, quoted in nearly every paper read in the Prophetic Conference, as a proof that the whole world is not to be converted under the dispensation of the Holy Spirit, but only a definite number — the Bride of Christ — is Rom. xi. 25. The word "fullness," Dr. E. R. Craven, and the millenarians generally, interpret as the completion of the definite "elect number of the Gentiles" who are to be saved; if but a thousand, then the nine hundred and ninety-nine saved persons lack but one to complete the fullness. Since quite a parade has been made of the great scholarship of the millenarians, we, in Pauline style, in self-defense, wish to magnify the scholarship on our side.

Our limits forbid giving Meyer's extended note. We insert only his conclusion: "A *part* of Israel is hardened, until the Gentiles *collectively* shall have come in, and when that shall have taken place, then *all* Israel will be saved. The conversion of the Gentiles ensues by successive stages; but when their *totality* shall be converted, then the conversion of the Jews in their *totality* will ensue; so that Paul sees the latter (which up to that epoch certainly also advances gradually in individual cases) ensuing, after the full conversion of the Gentiles, as the event completing the assemblage of the Church and accomplishing itself, probably, in rapid development. All this, therefore, is *before* the *Parousia* (personal coming), not *by means of* it." The italics are Meyer's. Turning to Dr. Robinson's Lexicon, we find him defining *pleroma* (fullness), in his text, as "all the multitude of the Gentiles." But lest Dr. Robinson may be considered obsolete, we turn to Cremer's Biblico-Theological Lexicon, 1878, fresh from the living author. His rendering is, "the *totality* or completeness of the Gentiles," under the same sub-heading of definitions as "the fullness of the God-head" — "*the sum total of all that God is.*" After this presentation of the latest and most erudite researches into the meaning of this text, the challenge of the Prophetic Conference to produce one proof-text for the conversion of the entire world under the present dispensation, does not exhibit an acquaintance with the best sacred scholarship of the age.

RESTITUTION OF ALL THINGS.

Another text, supposed beyond all dispute to contain an unanswerable proof of Chiliasm, is Acts iii. 21. We are told that "the restitution of all things" is the renovation of the earth at the second coming of Christ. But how can *all* things be restored so long as the vast majority of the dead are in their graves during a thousand years? The word "restitution" in the Greek is found nowhere else in the New Testament. It is, therefore, of doubtful meaning. But the cognate verb is used in Matt. xvii. 11: "Elias shall first come and *restore all things.*" Christ declares that "Elias has already come." But did he *restore* all things in the sense thrust upon the derivative noun by millenarians? John the Baptist as the forerunner of Christ *fulfilled all things* spoken concerning him by the prophets. Now read Acts iii. 21, substituting *fulfillment* for *restitution*, and see how complete is the sense and how perfect the harmony with the next verse: "Whom the heaven must receive until the times of the fulfillment of all things spoken of by the mouth of all his holy prophets since the world began. For Moses truly said unto the fathers," etc. Whatever is the meaning of the word "restitution," the work must be completed *before* Christ comes, not *by* His coming. Says Meyer: "Before the times set in which all things will be restored, Christ comes not from heaven. Consequently the age to come cannot be meant; but only such times as shall precede the *Parousia*, and by the emergence of which it is *conditioned* that the *Parousia* shall ensue." "Christ's reception into heaven continues — this is the idea of the apostle — until the moral corruption of the people of God is removed, and the thorough renovation of all their relations shall have ensued." Even Bengel can find no foothold for millenarianism in this speech of Peter. "Peter comprises the whole course of the times of the New Testament between the Ascension of the Lord and His Advent in glory, times in which that apostolic age shines forth pre-eminent (ver. 24), as also corresponding to the condition of the Church, which was to be constituted of Jews and Gentiles together. Just as Jonas says, 'Christ is that King, who has now received heaven, reigning in the meantime through the Gospel in the Spirit until all things be restored, *i. e.*, until the remainder of the Jews and Gentiles be converted.'" Bengel seems to endorse Jonas. This certainly teaches that the world is to be converted before the Advent, and not by it.

WHY CHRIST DELAYS HIS COMING.

Now let us turn to the third chapter of the second epistle of Peter for a commentary on his meaning in Acts iii. 21. He gives in this chapter an answer to the scoffers who say,

"Where is the (fulfilled) promise of His coming?" He then gives two reasons for Christ's delay in coming to burn up the earth and the works therein, namely: (1) The different conception of time in the divine Mind, a thousand years being as one day; and (2) the long-suffering of God in affording a further space for repentance. From this second reason the inference is irresistible that there will be no chance for repentance unto salvation after Christ's advent. If this be so, what becomes of the theory that He will come to supersede the dispensation of the Paraclete by the establishment of a dispensation in which Jews and Gentiles will be converted in a wholesale way?

If a thousand people were perishing on an ocean steamer wrecked at the entrance of the harbor of New York, and a small dory were rescuing two or three at a time while a well-equipped, life-saving government steamer was lying in sight of the wreck, could it be believed that the commander delayed to hasten to help the unfortunate, through his excessive compassion for them? This is the exact attitude of Christ towards a perishing world according to millenarianism, purposing to institute a dispensation more favorable to the salvation of the lost world, and delaying out of pity!

When we ask why does Christ delay His coming to set up a more effective scheme of salvation, we are told that this question is like the conundrum, why did not God create the world sooner? But Peter has answered our question in a way which grinds millenarianism to powder. He delays through a long-suffering which implies that He will come, not to save, but to condemn; not to set up a visible kingdom on the earth, but to wind up His mediatorial reign and deliver up the kingdom to God, even the Father. This is what St. Paul avers will be done at the second advent (1 Cor. xv. 23, 24). Also contrast John iii. 16, 17; xii. 47, with Matt. xxv. 31–46; 2 Thess. i. 6–10.

Conclusion.

I have discussed this subject from a sense of duty to my fellow-Christians. I believe that the general prevalence of pre-millennialism would be disastrous to the best interests of the Kingdom of Christ, now being spread over the earth by the joint agency of the Holy Spirit and consecrated believers. The command, "Grieve not the Spirit," cannot be fully kept by any person whose theories belittle His efficiency in the work of His office. Nor can any man put forth his best endeavors while distrusting the agency with which he co-works and looking for a superior one soon to appear. Against all the disclaimers of diminished zeal for the evangelization of the whole world, put forth by pessimists of the Second Advent school, they fail to convince me that men, however good, will ever exert themselves to the utmost to prove themselves false prophets.

This is contrary to human nature even in its highest state of grace. Gen. Grant would have failed to conquer Gen. Lee, if he had believed it impossible.

As to the premillennial features discussed in this work, no more fitting words in conclusion can be given than those with which David Brown (of Jamieson, Fausett, and Brown fame) closes the Fourth Edition of his "Christ's Second Coming" (procurable second hand of James Robinson, Manchester, Eng.):—

"I have shown, I think, under a number of heads, that the premillennial scheme is at variance with the Word of God; that it proceeds upon crude and arbitrary principles of interpretation, while it shrinks from carrying out even these to their legitimate results; that as a system it wants coherence, and is palpably defective, making no provision for some of the most important events which are to occur in the history of the race; and that its bearing on some of the most precious doctrines of God's Word is painful and perilous.

"These are strong things to say. Could I have taken the view of this system which many do who never examined it, — that it is a harmless one, which it matters little whether we embrace or reject, — I have too much dislike to oppose brethren in the common salvation to have sent forth such a volume as this. It is because I saw in it ELEMENTS WHICH AT ONCE FASCINATE THE CARNAL AND ATTRACT THE SPIRITUAL that I thought it of consequence to sift it."

APPENDIX

CONTAINING

CHRIST'S COMINGS:

I. WAS WESLEY A PREMILLENNIALIST?
II. CHRIST'S PRELIMINARY AND MILLENNIAL COMINGS COMPARED AND IDENTIFIED:
  1. *Christ's Preliminary Comings.*
  2. *Christ's Millennial Coming.*
III. THE WORLD'S CONVERSION AFTER CHRIST'S SECOND ADVENT IMPOSSIBLE.

BY THE
REV. CHARLES MUNGER.

ANTINOMIANISM CHARACTERIZED.
BY THE
REV. ROBERT HALL, A.M.
LONG-TIME PASTOR OF THE BAPTIST CHURCH IN BRISTOL, ENG.

AND OTHER UTTERANCES.

"WAS WESLEY A PREMILLENNIALIST?"

"What can we say, but that ingenious men have strange dreams; and these they sometimes mistake for realities." — John Wesley.

It has been said that John Wesley was a premillennialist; that he contended for that faith, none more earnestly; that Methodism once grasped and utilized it with power; yea, that its "foundations were laid deep in the premillennial faith of the pure apostolic and primitive church."

In support of these assertions the writer appeals to Tyerman. Tyerman does say that Wesley endorsed the doctrine "that at Christ's second coming the martyrs will be raised, and for a thousand years will reign with Christ in Jerusalem," and that that reign will be visible. But he also says in the same place: "This is a matter which none of Wesley's biographers have noticed."

There were six biographers of Wesley before Tyerman. And as he makes no claim to the discovery of any new facts touching this matter, the presumption is as six to one that Tyerman was wrong just then, for if the facts were as above related, they were of very great importance, and it is not supposable that six men would ignore them. The writer above quoted, and also Tyerman, appeal to a certain letter as proof of Wesley's premillennial faith. Does that letter contain what they say it does? Here is what they report of it:—

"The doctrine which Justin deduced from the prophets and apostles, and in which he was undoubtedly followed by the Fathers of the second and third centuries, is this: the souls of them who have been martyred for the witness of Jesus, and for the Word of God, and of those who have not worshipped the beast, neither received his mark, shall live and reign with Christ a thousand years. But the rest of the dead lived not again until the thousand years are finished. Now to say that they (the Fathers) believe this, is neither more nor less than to say they believe the Bible."

Does this letter say a word about Christ's second coming, or His visible reign, or the reign of the saints in Jerusalem? Not a word of it is said or implied. On Rev. xx. 4, Wesley says: "They reigned with Christ not on earth, but in heaven." How does their reign with Christ in heaven prove either His or their reign in Jerusalem or on earth? Were not those ingenious men "dreaming" when they thought they found premillennialism in that letter?

The writer above quoted appeals to Wesley's commendation of a book in which premillennialism is taught, and also to Tyerman's declaration that Wesley held "in substance" the opinions of its author. Tyerman names four of the author's "chief points," three of which any post-millennialist may hold, and so "in substance" may agree with him though differing at the point at issue in this discussion. Wesley, in his "Notes on the New Testament," followed Bengel largely but definitely on the nearness of the binding of Satan and the millennium; also in the opinion that Rev. xx. 1–11 included two thousand years, in the first of which Satan will be bound and the church and world will have "immunity from all evils and an affluence of all blessings" — the millennium. During the second thousand years Satan will be loosed, and "while the saints reign with Christ in heaven, men on earth will be careless and secure." After this second thousand years, according to Wesley, the second advent will occur. His words are unequivocal and decisive: "Quickly he [Satan] will be bound; when he is loosed the martyrs will live and reign with Christ. Then follows His coming in glory" (Notes on Rev. xx. 1-11). So, in his sermon on "The Great Assize," Wesley distinctly places the second advent at the judgment (Rev. xx. 11-15), which the apostle says and all admit is after the millennium. These facts show conclusively that Wesley placed the second advent after the millennium. And in this he parted from Bengel, if, as alleged, he placed the advent before the millennium.

Partisan criticism has torn some of Wesley's expressions from their connections and twisted them from their intent, to give the impression that he was a Universalist. So on this subject, expressions may be found in his popular addresses which, literally interpreted, would make him appear to teach what he never intended. Sober criticism

"WAS WESLEY A PREMILLENNIALIST?" 275

tests such expressions by his uniform and exposi tional teaching. Premillennialists think they find their peculiarities in certain texts. But in almost every text Wesley negatives their expositions. Below are a few examples. The figures '78, '86, refer to the reports of the Prophetic Conferences of 1878 and 1886, which may be taken as the best accredited representation of premillennial thought of Europe and America. The letter S. refers to Rev. A. B. Simpson's "Gospel of the Kingdom." References to Wesley are to his "Notes on the New Testament," and his sermons.

MODERN PREMILLENNIALISM.	JOHN WESLEY.
Christ's second advent, before the millennium ('86, p. 43).	After the millennium (notes on Rev. xx. 1-11; x. 7. Sermons vol. 1, pp. 126-135, 454).
Christ comes the second time to	
1. Set up His kingdom — a temporal kingdom ('86, pp. 149, 177).	It was set up at His first advent (On Matt. xvi. 28; Mark i. 15; ix. 1). A temporal kingdom a "dream" (On Acts i. 6).
2. To convert the world ('78, p. 8).	To judge the world (On Matt. xxv. 31-46).

3. To open a new dispensation of grace and missions ('86, pp. 31, 37).	The present "the last dispensation of grace" (On 1 John ii. 18).
4. "To steal away His waiting church," not all saints, but His bride, "elect within the elect," into "the air" to "the marriage of the Lamb" (S., pp. 120, 221).	To take "believers of all ages . . . in the same moment to be with the Lord in heaven" (On 1 Thess. iv. 15, 17).
The conversion of the world "only at and by the return of Christ" ('78, p. 8).	"Thus will the Gospel leaven the world" (On Matt. xix. 33).
The leaven, Matt. xiii. 33, means corruption, apostasy ('78, p. 209. S., p. 10).	It means the gospel of Christ (On Matt. xiii. 33).
The foolish virgins "not lost, but they lose something" (S., p. 53).	"Those poor wretches who had so long deceived . . . their own souls. . . . Oh, no! the time is past and returns no more" (On Matt. xxv. 9).
Christ will rebuild the kingdom of David and "enter upon the kingdom" at His second advent ('78, p. 490; '86, p. 149).	"The kingdom of the Messiah was spiritual, not temporal." "It came with power at Pentecost." "Look not for it in distant times, it is come, it is present in the souls of believers" (On Acts xxviii. 23; Luke xvii. 21; Mark ix. 1).
Then the Jews will be chief of the nations and reign as princes ('78, p. 236; '86, p. 122; S., p. 12).	A temporal kingdom in which the Jews should have dominion over the nations — a dream (On Acts i. 6).

"WAS WESLEY A PREMILLENNIALIST?" 277

There are different judgments, some say three, others, four ('86, p. 114; S., p. 227).	One judgment universal and eternal (Ser. I., pp. 126–135, 454).
The judgment of Matt. xxv. 31–46 is not that of Rev. xx. 11–15 ('78, p. 252).	The same (Ser. I., pp. 129, 454).
"The believer shall not come into judgment" that of Rev. xx. 11–15 ('78, p. 308; '86, p. 114).	They will be the first judged at that judgment (Ser. I. p. 131).
The purpose of God is not to convert the world in this dispensation ('78, p. 281; '86, p. 37).	"The design of Christ's commission" was to "make disciples of all nations" (On Matt. xxviii. 19; Mark xvi. 15).
Saints only will be raised at the second advent ('78, pp. 84, 102, 308).	Every human being will then be raised (Ser. I, p. 129).
Saints literally eating and drinking "ambrosial viands" at Christ's table, and sitting on thrones, etc. ('78, pp. 180, 227, 265).	These are "figurative terms" respecting "the spiritual honors and delights of Christ's kingdom of grace and glory" (On Luke xxii. 30).
The earth will be burned (2 Peter, iii. 7–12), but "after the fire there will still be nations in the flesh." "The earth and Israel will remain" ('86, p. 149).	"The heavens and the earth"—the universe—will pass away; "no place was found for them," "they ceased to exist, they were no more" (On 2 Peter iii. 7–12; Rev. xx. 11). [How Israel and the nations *in the flesh* will dodge this fire, they have not said.]

The above is a fair but by no means a full exhibit of the antagonism of Wesley to modern premillennialism. Mr. Simpson's notions about bridal company and the wedding in the air at which some of the saved will not be wedded; about the Jews mourning as they see Christ's train sweep by and leave them; about the New Jerusalem, "a solid cube" "376 miles each way," "poised just above the earth;" about the enormous increase of population after the advent, necessitating perhaps a colonization of "stars" over which some of "the true and tried will be rulers with a whole world to love and bless;" have not been inserted in the above list, for probably they are his own "whimsies," not endorsed outside of his following. But the points above named sufficiently indicate the substance of the best accredited type of modern premillennialism, concerning which be it remembered that Wesley never taught a single point named above; that his teaching is opposed to every one; that Methodism never had anything to do with premillennialism, ancient or modern, but to antagonize it.

It is claimed that premillennialism was the

faith of the primitive church for three hundred years. I reply: —

1. An essential factor of the premillennialism which we are examining is the belief that the world is to be converted at, by, or after Christ's second advent. Eliminate this doctrine from the schemes of the Prophetic Conferences and of Mr. Simpson, and they cease to be what they are.

But there is no evidence, even from their own witnesses, that that belief was ever the faith of the primitive church, or any part of that faith — not even of the premillennialists themselves. Not one of their witnesses testifies to any such thing. They testify to the prevalence of ancient premillennialists which, bating its whims, which premillennialism never mention now, was "for substance" the belief that Christ was soon coming to reign visibly at Jerusalem and those who had believed on Him would be made immortal and reign with Him a thousand years on earth in the enjoyment of physical and spiritual delights. Comparing this with the doctrines above stated, it is apparent that the ancient and modern types are so radically unlike that all argument from that for this is sophistical.

2. As to the ancient type called chiliasm and its prevalence, the following facts are distinctly attested by the authorities named: "That the Jews were to enjoy a thousand years of glory upon the renovated earth under the reign of Messiah, who was soon to appear at Jerusalem, to raise their dead and expel and destroy their oppressors, was a prevalent belief at the time of Christ" (Milman). "This notion in a modified form passed over to the Christians" (Neander), "was accepted in its modified form by many and was rejected by many orthodox Christians" (Justin). "It never was the faith of the primitive church" (Neander), "nor a test of orthodoxy" (Schlegel). "Its flourishing period was about one hundred years" (Shedd). "It began to decline about the middle of the third century" (Mosheim). At the close of that century it "seems to have been generally abandoned" (Burton). Among the causes of its abandonment were its "unspiritual excesses" (Alford), its "gross carnalism" (Jamieson and Fausset, premillennialists). It produced divisions and apostasies of whole churches" (Eusebius). "When tested by the Scriptures it

collapsed" (Dionysius). "There is not a trace of it in any summary of Christian doctrines during the first three hundred years, not even in those written by premillennialists, Justin, Ireneus, Tertullian. Heretics were very fond of it, were the first to preach it among nominal Christians, and the last to quit it" (Burton).

3. Of the historians who lived in either of the first five hundred years, not one has yet been found who even intimates that premillennialism was ever the faith of the primitive church. It has appeared frequently in church history, only to work mischief wherever it obtained organic form. Its present type is born of doubt, feeds on doubt, and generates doubt as to God's purpose and plan touching the conversion of the world. This doubt by the perversion of language is called "faith." As in the past, when time has shown its falsity the wreckage of souls will be lamentable.

Zion's Herald.

CHRIST'S PRELIMINARY AND MILLENNIAL COMINGS COMPARED AND IDENTIFIED.

I. Christ's Preliminary Comings.

MODERN premillennialism is unscriptural in its views of Christ's millennial coming and of the millennium.

Its views of Christ's millennial coming are unscriptural in these particulars, viz.: That it will be in the body; that it was imminent 1800 years ago; that it is now imminent; that it will be the panacea for all political and social evils, and will introduce a new dispensation for the conversion of the world, or of such remnants of the nations as somehow shall have escaped the fiery judgments of His second advent.

That Christ will come again in like manner as He went up into heaven, has ever been, and, with individual exception, is now the faith of the Church. But the Scriptures plainly teach other comings of the Lord Christ, and other modes of coming.

The argument here is: —

1. Christ is the Lord in both Testaments, the Old and the New.

2. Christ the Lord has often come potentially in extraordinary mercies and judgments.

3. His millennial coming will be of this class.

The first proposition is conceded by evangelical Christians, and needs no proof here. The second and third are to be proven from the Scriptures.

To understand the prophets we must consider their terms, style, and time.

God is said to be everywhere. Yet the inspired writers speak of His absence; His coming and going; His forsaking and returning.

God is a spirit. But often He is represented as having the members of a human body, and as acting as a man, and even as a lion, a bear, a bird. As a man of war He has a camp, an army to which He utters His voice, and which He musters to battle. Of men is His army sometimes composed, but in Joel, ii. 11, 25, it is of locusts, caterpillars and worms. He rises up and goes before His army. He lays siege to cities and destroys them, while others He defends and delivers.

If now an extreme literalist who boasts that he takes the Bible just as it reads, interpret these representations in a materialistic sense, and accept the idea that God is a great man, consistency demands that when He is spoken of as acting as a lion, a bear, a bird, he should devoutly believe and confess that his God is a real beast or bird.

But sober criticism finds itself compelled to interpret these terms mataphorically, the key thereto being the two little words "as if." God has done and will do "as if" a man, a lion, a bear, did thus. In Hosea xii. 10, God says: "I have spoken by the prophets, and I have multiplied visions, and used similitudes, by the ministry of the prophets."

This shows that God is represented as saying and doing what His agents say and do by His inspiration, and also that His prophets and teachers by His inspiration used similitudes. This premillennialists themselves admit — on occasions. Thus, for example, Doctors Jamieson and Fausset, on Ezek. xxxviii, say: —

"The prophetic delineations of the Saviour's principles of government are thrown into the familiar forms of Old Testament relations. The final triumph of the Messiah's truth over the distant nations is represented as a literal conflict, on a gigantic scale, Israel being the battle-field. It is a prophetic parable, *i. e.*, similitude."

Personality and materiality are by no means identical. God is a spiritual personality, but not a material person. So when we speak of the personal coming and reign of Christ, we do not necessarily mean his bodily coming and reign. In addition to, and vastly different from, Christ's first and second bodily descents from heaven, the Scriptures frequently speak of other comings, and of these, two classes occupy chiefly the attention of the sacred writers, viz: His spiritual and judicial comings.

These are not limited to any dispensation, but are common to all, not peculiar to prophecy but frequent in history, and that the history of individuals and of the Church, as well as of cities and nations. Consider a few cases of His coming and dwelling upon the earth.

"I will come and dwell among you," was the supreme promise and bliss of the old covenant, Ex. xxix. 42–46. "I dwell in the high and holy place, with him also that is of a contrite and humble spirit," Is., lvii. 15. The supreme promise of the New Testament is: "If a man love me, he will keep my word; and my Father will love him, and we will come unto him, and make our abode with him," John xiv. 23. "If any man hear my voice and open the door, I will come in to him, and will sup with him, and he with me," Rev. iii. 20.

But this glory — God with man — was too great to be apprehended without sensible manifestation. Hence the pillar of fire and cloud at the opening of the Mosaic dispensation, and through the forming period of the Jewish Church, and its occasional appearance in their history to the sad hour of its departure from the Temple, just before both were given over to the desolation of the Babylonian captivity. Hence also the return of that "Glory of the Lord" at the birth of Christ and at Pentecost. The appearing of that fiery token was the recognized sign of God's presence — the Epiphany — the manifestation of His presence.

At the dedication of the Tabernacle Moses said: "To-day the Lord will appear," and immediately changed the expression to "The glory of the Lord shall appear unto you" (Lev. ix. 4–6). The Holy Spirit was the executive of the Godhead as truly in the Jewish, as He is in the Christian Church. God left them and returned to them and abode with them by the Holy Spirit — "His presence."

But this "Glory of the Lord," — this same fiery cloudy pillar — had also its dark side, the symbol of woe. It was a cloud of darkness to the Egyptians, but it gave light to His people. In the morning watch the Lord looked upon the Egyptians through the fiery cloud, and they fled to their doom, crying: "The Lord fighteth against the Egyptians" (Ex. xiv. 19–25).

Here at the very beginning of the history of the Church is an example and key to all subsequent prophetic visions which represent God as fighting for His people against their enemies. Hence the Psalmist, xcvii. 1–5: —

"The Lord reigneth. . . .
Clouds and darkness are round about him;
Righteousness and judgment are the foundation of His throne.

A fire goeth before him,
And burneth up His adversaries round about.
His lightnings lightened the world:
The earth saw, and trembled.
The hills melted like wax at the presence of the Lord."

In Is. lxiv. 3, God's action is spoken of as a "coming":—

"When Thou didst terrible things which we looked not for,
Thou camest down, the mountains flowed down at thy presence.

To Moses, God said: "I have seen the affliction of my people in Egypt, and am come down to deliver them." Later He added: "I will pass through the land of Egypt this night, and will smite all the first-born." And he did. How? By His death angel, the plague. To Israel, God said: "When I see the blood I will pass over you." And he did. How? By exempting them from the plague, as He said: "The plague shall not be upon you to destroy you, when I smite the land of Egypt."

Another example is in the destruction of Samaria and the Northern Kingdom, B.C. 721, and the deliverance of Jerusalem and Judah soon after. The

CHRIST'S PRELIMINARY COMINGS. 289

Samaritan Kingdom began in sin, and had been a constant menace to God's cause and people. God warned them by His prophets, and they represented that destruction as His leaving them and coming in judgments.

By Hosea, God said: "I will be unto Ephraim as a lion. . . . I, even I, will tear and go away. . . . I will go and return to my place, till they acknowledge their offence" (v. 14–15).

By Amos: "I will pass through the midst of thee," "and because I will do this unto thee, prepare to meet thy God, O Israel" (v. 7, and iv. 12).

By Micah: "The Lord cometh forth out of His place, and will come down, and tread upon the high places of the earth. And the mountains shall be molten under Him, and the valleys shall be cleft, as wax before the fire. . . . Therefore I will make Samaria as an heap of the field" (i. 3–6).

Last of all Isaiah gave warning, and described the mode: "The Lord shall rise up as in Mount Perazim" (xxviii. 21). And how did the Lord rise up in Perazim? The allusion is to the overthrow of the Philistines gathered to dispute David's sovereignty, in 1 Chr. xiv. 9–17. To David's inquiry,

God said: "When thou hearest the sound of marching in the tops of the mulberry-trees, then shalt thou go out to battle; for God is gone out before thee to smite the host of the Philistines." David obeyed, and declared of the event: "God hath broken mine enemies by mine hand, like the breach of waters." God does what His agents do at His command.

All these predictions of God's destructive "comings" to Samaria and its Kingdom were fulfilled within a few years of Isaiah's warning. How? By the Assyrian armies, who made Samaria desolate and destroyed the Northern Kingdom. Thus did the Lord come down and tread upon "the high places of the earth," and punish the apostate people.

But another side was there to Micah's prophecy, a mercy side of the Lord's coming. Micah had said in the symbolic style of the prophets: "The Lord will come down. And the mountains shall be molten under Him, and the valleys shall be cleft, as wax before the fire." Having destroyed the Northern Kingdom the Assyrians turned to Southern Palestine, and having wasted it, threatened Jerusalem.

CHRIST'S PRELIMINARY COMINGS. 291

In this situation the perils to God's church were depicted as mountains. Hezekiah and his people were as kids in the paw of the lion. But they cried to God, and Isaiah thus records his prayer: —

> "Oh Lord! . . .
> Return for Thy servants' sake. . . .
> Oh that Thou wouldest rend the heavens, that Thou wouldest come down,"
> "That the mountains might flow down at thy presence, . . .
> To make Thy name known to thine adversaries,
> That the nations may tremble at Thy presence."
> (Is. lxiii. 17, and lxiv. 1-3.)

Is there a passage in all the Scriptures which seems more explicitly to assert a literal coming of the Lord than does this? But did the prophet really mean that the God-man Jesus Christ would actually rend the heavens and visibly appear? Not if one will read the next sentence: —

> "When Thou did'st terrible things which we looked not for,
> Thou camest down, the mountains flowed down at Thy presence."

Will the literalist attempt to show when and

where the God-man came down, and the material mountains flowed down at his presence? Did God answer that prayer? He did, having first promised: —

> "Like as when the lion growleth and the young lion over his prey, . . .
> So shall the Lord of Hosts come down to fight upon Mount Zion,
> And upon the hill thereof.
> As birds flying, so will the Lord of Hosts protect Jerusalem;
> He will protect and deliver it."

Repeated was this promise, and its fulfilment recorded, by Isaiah (xxxvii. 35–36): —

> "I will defend this city to save it,
> For mine own sake, and for my servant David's sake."

"And the angel of the Lord went forth, and smote in the camp of the Assyrians a hundred and fourscore and five thousand." Here was an exact fulfilment of the promise, "The Lord of Hosts shall come down to fight upon Mount Zion; He will protect and deliver it." How? Not in the person of the God-man, but by His death angel. According to Hibbard, Houbigant, Hengstenberg, and Alexander, Psalm xlvi. was written in commemoration of this overthrow of Sennacherib. Read it and see how inspiration speaks of that event:—

> "God is our refuge and strength,
> A very present help in trouble.
> Therefore will we not fear, though the earth do change,
> And though the mountains be moved in the heart of the seas; . . .
>
> The nations raged, the kingdoms were moved:
> He uttered His voice, the earth melted.
> The Lord of Hosts is with us:
> The God of Jacob is our refuge."

Another example of God's judicial withdrawing and returning is in the prophecy and history of the Babylonian exile and restoration. That history shows:—

1. God leaving His people, and delivering them to punishment in Babylon.

2. God returning and reigning over them at Jerusalem.

3. God coming to punish Babylon, and thus redeeming His people Zion by visiting terrible things on their enemies.

Isaiah had said (i. 27): "Zion shall be redeemed with judgment." Not now by the blood of the covenant, but by the blood of her oppressors. Look at the testimony in its order of time. Because of their irreclaimable apostasy, God said:—

... "I will utterly forget you,
And I will cast you off,
And the city that I gave unto you and to your fathers,
Away from my presence." (Jer. xxiii. 39.)

Eleven years later the Lord gave to Ezekiel a view of the visible sign of His presence departing from the Holy of Holies, to the gate of the Temple, then over the city, and then from the city. What did this mean? God answered (Jer. xii. 7):—

"I have forsaken my house,
 I have cast off my heritage;
 I have given the dearly beloved of my soul into the hand of her enemies."

So Jeremiah understood it, for in tears he wrote (vii. 29): "The Lord hath rejected and forsaken the generation of His wrath." To that whole generation this meant the suspension of all saving power in their sacrifices and offerings, with the cessation of answers to their prayer, in these terrible words (Jer. xiv. 10–12): —

> "Pray not for this people for their good.
> When they fast — I will not hear their cry;
> And when they offer burnt offering and oblation — I will not accept them.
> But I will consume them by the sword,
> And by the famine, and by the pestilence."

This was God's answer to the prayer of agony wrung from the heart of Jeremiah: "O Lord, leave us not!" This meant that their day of mercy as a nation was passed, and their day of judgment at hand. God's bribeless executioners, war, pestilence, and famine were beginning their work of retribution.

But a remnant was true to God. By a vision it was made known that though they might go to Babylon with the bad, yet because of their integrity it should be for their good. To such He said (Jer. xxiv. 1–7): —

> "I will bring them again to this land;
> And I will build them, . . .
> And I will plant them, . . .

And I will give them a heart to know me, that I am
    the Lord ;
And they shall be my people, and I will be their God ;
For they shall return unto me with their whole heart."

Repeated was this promise (Jer. xxix. 10–13) : —

" After seventy years be accomplished for Babylon,
I will visit you, and perform my good word toward you,
In causing you to return to this place. . . .
And ye shall seek me, and find me,
When ye shall search for me with all your heart."

This was the hope of the Church in Babylon all the dreary years of that captivity, and just one year before the edict of restoration the Spirit of God touched the heart of His Psalmist, and he wrote (Ps. l. 3–5) : —

" Our God shall come, . . .
He shall call to the heavens above,
And to the earth, . . .
Gather my saints together unto me."

Similarly another (cii. 13) : —

" Thou shalt arise and have mercy upon Zion ;
For it is time to have pity upon her, yea, the set time
    is come."

Shortly came the decree for the restoration, B.C. 536, and soon the returning exiles were building at Jerusalem, though many remained in Babylon. Then by the prophet (Zech. ii. 6–10) God sent to them this call: —

> "Ho, ho,
> Flee from the land of the north, saith the Lord; . . .
> Ho, Zion, escape,
> Thou that dwellest with the daughter of Babylon. . .
> Sing and rejoice, O daughter of Zion;
> For, lo, I come,
> And I will dwell in the midst of thee, saith the Lord."

In the same year, according to Bagster's chronology, B.C. 519, God spake to this same prophet (Zech. i. 16–17): —

> "I am returned to Jerusalem with mercies;
> My house shall be built in it, saith the Lord of Hosts, . . .
> My cities through prosperity shall yet be spread abroad;
> And the Lord shall yet comfort Zion,
> And shall yet choose Jerusalem."

A year later this is repeated (Zech. viii. 3): —

> "I am returned unto Zion,
> And will dwell in the midst of Jerusalem."

The glory of this revelation of God to His church is unfolded in the same chapter, and its effect upon the heathen, the nations, is thus announced. Men of all nations will say (Zech. viii. 23): "We will go with you, for we have heard that God is with you."

Here is a coming of the Lord, and His presence with His people, and His dwelling and reigning with and over them at Jerusalem and the cities round about. This all results in the awakening and attraction of men of all languages to them by the manifested presence of God with them.

Will any one affirm this to refer to the material presence, the bodily coming of the God-man, he must do so in direct contradiction to God's own explanation of the case by the prophet Haggai, who was an actor at the time. (Hag. ii. 15.) As they were building at Jerusalem, the word of the Lord came to them, thus:—

"Be strong, O Zerubbabel, saith the Lord;
   And be strong, O Joshua, son of Jehozadak, the high priest;
   And be strong, all ye people of the land, saith the Lord, and work;

For I am with you, saith the Lord of Hosts;
According to the word that I covenanted with you
When ye came out of Egypt.
And my spirit abideth (*marg.*) among you;
Fear ye not."

This covenant upon coming out of Egypt was in these words: "My presence shall go with you;" and here He says that, according to that covenant, He was with the builders at Jerusalem under Zerubbabel, and that He had come by His Spirit to build up Zion.

But consider also the dark side of this coming of the Lord. God said He would visit Babylon, and He did by terrible things, and this was the retributive side of His coming at the restoration or redemption of His people from their captivity in Babylon (Hag. ii. 21, 22).

By Jeremiah (l. 31, 32) God said to Babylon:—

"Thy day is come, the time that I will visit thee.
And the proud one shall stumble and fall."

Similarly Isaiah (xiii. 1, 5) : —

"The Lord of Hosts mustereth the host for battle.
They come from a far country.

> From the uttermost part of heaven,
> Even the Lord, and the weapons of His indignation,
> To destroy the whole land."

Who come? "The Lord and the weapons of His indignation." Who were the weapons of His indignation? Verse 17 answers: "I will stir up the Medes against them. . . . And Babylon . . . shall be as when God overthrew Sodom and Gomorrah" (19).

God mentioned the leader of that army by name, His "Mashiah," or "Christ," Cyrus, and said: "I will go before thee." And he did. How? Not by the God-man in visible presence, but in those "terrible things" which desolated Babylon and "all the kingdoms of the world" (Jer. xxv. 26), in which catastrophes the cities of the nations fell, empires and thrones and kingdoms were wiped out, and the trembling earth was deluged with blood.

Another prediction of Christ's potential coming is in Mal. iii. 1–5: —

> "And the Lord, whom ye seek,
> Shall suddenly come to His temple; . . .
> And He shall purify the sons of Levi, . . .
> And they shall offer unto the Lord offerings in righteousness.

CHRIST'S PRELIMINARY COMINGS. 301

> Then shall the offering of Judah and Jerusalem
> Be pleasant unto the Lord,
> As in the days of old."

Here, as often, Old Testament terms are used to set forth New Testament facts. The application of the passage to Christ and His work is beyond dispute. Its misapplication to His coming and work in Herod's Temple has blinded many. The facts are that He was not the Lord whom the Jews were seeking; that He did not purify the Levitical priesthood, only a mere fraction; and that the offerings of Judah and Jerusalem were not more acceptable to the Lord, but vastly more offensive because of their rejection of Him.

On the other hand, at Pentecost Christ by the Spirit did come and purify His Temple — the body of believers — and their offerings were in righteousness and acceptable unto the Lord as in days of old. Here was a Pentecostal coming of the Lord, and by it the extraordinary increase and establishment of His Kingdom.

But beside the mercy side of that coming, there was another — the punitive, in Mal. iii. 5: —

"And I will come near to you to judgment;
And I will be a swift witness against . . . (them
That) fear not Me, saith the Lord of Hosts."

In the parable of the wicked husbandmen (Mk. xii. 1–9), Christ exposed the Jewish Hierarchy, and said to them: "The Lord of the vineyard will come and destroy the husbandmen, and will give the vineyard to others." And this He did in that generation.

These various preliminary comings of the Lord Christ cover a period of fifteen hundred years. In each of them the following facts stand forth:—

1. An extraordinary evil or peril.

2. An extraordinary deliverance, and that by special divine intervention.

3. This intervention is called a "coming of the Lord."

4. In neither of them was there a coming of the man Christ Jesus.

5. Said comings are described by terms and symbols which cannot be interpreted in a material, literal sense.

Thus, it was not the man Christ Jesus who came

down and passed through Egypt; who came down
and trod upon the high places of the earth at
the destruction of Samaria; who fought for and
delivered Jerusalem by the destruction of Sennacherib; who came with Cyrus and the Medes to
redeem the exiles by the destruction of Babylon;
who returned to and dwelt in Jerusalem after the
Restoration; and who came and destroyed those
wicked husbandmen in the desolation of Palestine
by the Romans from A.D. 70–135.

It was not the literal mountains and hills that
skipped like lambs, when God came from Sinai
with His saints, who sat at His feet as pupils to
learn His Law. It was not the man Christ Jesus
who "bowed the heavens, and came down and rode
upon a cherub and did fly" to deliver David (2 Sam.
xxii. 10–18). It was not the material heavens
which were dissolved, — rolled together as a scroll,
— nor did their host fall down as the leaf falleth
off from the vine, on the day when God had "a
sacrifice in Bozrah, and a great slaughter in the
land of Idumea" (Is. xxxiv. 1–6).

So much upon the fatal results of misunderstanding figurative language.

II. Christ's Millennial Coming.

We are now prepared to examine the Scriptures which speak of that coming of Christ which belongs to the triumphant period of His Kingdom. Surprisingly few are they, considering the extraordinary claims of premillennialists.

Our argument rests only upon those which are acknowledged by both parties as millennial passages.

Agreed are both parties that Ps. lxxii. speaks of Christ's coming and the triumphant epoch of His Kingdom, when "the mountains" — governments — "shall bring peace to the people," when He "shall break in pieces the oppressor," and when "all kings shall fall down before him; all nations shall serve him." In verse 6 it does say "He shall come," and in verse 8, "He shall have dominion also from sea to sea, and from the River unto the ends of the earth."

What more could heart wish to prove beyond question the premillennial coming of Christ? Nothing but another glance at the rest of the text: —

"He shall come down *like rain upon the mown grass;*
As showers that water the earth."

Whether one and the same thing, or different things, are here spoken of, this is certain: Rain is never the symbol of the bodily coming of Christ. In Scripture, rain, water, showers are usually symbols of blessing: —

"And He shall come unto us as the rain,
As the latter rain that watereth the earth." (Hos. vi. 3.)

". . . It is time to seek the Lord,
Till He come and rain righteousness upon you." (Hos. x. 12.)

". . . I will pour water upon him that is thirsty,
And streams upon the dry ground;"

this being immediately explained as meaning: —

"I will pour my spirit upon thy seed,
And my blessing upon thine offspring:
And they shall spring up among the grass,
As willows by the watercourses." (Is. xliv. 3–4.)

"There shall be showers of blessing." (Ezek. xxxiv. 26.)

"I will be as the dew unto Israel.
He shall blossom as the lily." (Hos. xiv. 5.)

These are millennial promises, and, if the text of Ps. lxxii. 6 speaks of one fact only, then the coming of Christ there mentioned is plainly His coming by the Holy Spirit, as predicted by Isaiah, Ezekiel, and Christ. This settles the question, and shows that Christ's millennial coming is by the Holy Spirit, and is not a visible bodily coming, for no sane man would use the term "like rain" to denote a bodily coming.

But more than "blessing" is indicated by the terms of the text. "He shall come down like rain upon the *mown* grass" is not a natural symbol of "showers of blessing." Rain upon the *mown* grass means damage — destruction. Mowing is not a symbol of blessing, but of calamity. Vitringa and others aver that: "The metaphor of mowing or reaping is used in most authors to signify an excision or utter destruction of the subject."

So in Scripture rain is a symbol of evil.

"Upon the wicked He shall rain snares." (Ps. xi. 6.)

"And I will call for a sword against him . . .
And I will plead against him with pestilence and blood;

> And I will rain upon him, and upon his hordes,
> And upon the many peoples that are with him,
> An overflowing shower, and great hailstones, fire and brimstone.
> And I will magnify myself, and sanctify myself,
> And I will make myself known in the eyes of many nations,
> And they shall know that I am the Lord." (Ezek. xxxviii. 21-23.)

Similarly Christ: "The rain descended, and the floods came . . . and smote upon that house; and it fell." (Matt. vii. 27.)

So in this millennial psalm, "He comes," not only in "showers of blessing," but —

> "He shall break in pieces the oppressor." (v. 5.)
> "And his enemies shall lick the dust." (v. 9.)

Most plainly there is not the slightest intimation of the bodily coming of Christ in this confessedly millennial psalm. On the contrary the two factors of His preliminary coming with power are distinctly asserted.

Another passage which connects a coming of Christ and the triumph of His Kingdom is Is. lix. 16 to lxiii. 12 inclusive. Herein are the same two factors of His historic or preliminary comings with power: —

1. A great peril — the enemy coming in like a flood. (lix. 19.)
2. The Spirit of the Lord lifts up a standard against him — "shall put him to flight."(Jamieson.)
3. "A redeemer shall come to Zion, and unto them that turn from transgression in Jacob."
4. This is God's covenant with them — Zion and Jacob. (lix. 21.)
5. Thus the Lord as the sun of righteousness "shall arise upon Zion, and His glory shall be seen upon her." (lx. 2.)
6. Thus and then "the nations shall come to thy light, and kings to the brightness of thy rising." (lx. 3.)

Premillennialists see in this the second advent of Christ in the body to restore the Jews and destroy the Gentiles, — the living nations, — and after this the millennial glory. The prophet says: "The enemy shall come in like a flood," but it is "the Spirit of the Lord"[*] — not the man Christ Jesus — which shall put him to flight.

[*] This is the reading of the A. V. and the margin of the R. V.

"A redeemer shall come to Zion, and to them that turn from transgression in Jacob." Whence? from heaven? Not a word of it. Of this very case Paul said: —

"There shall come out of Zion the Deliverer:
He shall turn away ungodliness from Jacob;
And this is my covenant unto them." (Rom. xi. 26, 27.)

This covenant is reported by Is. lix. 21, by Jer. xxxi. 31, 34, and in the Writer to the Hebrews (viii. 1–13; x. 15–17). If now the premillennialists have found a single word in either of those inspired reports, as to the Redeemer's coming from heaven in body to Zion or out of Zion — to turn away ungodliness from Jacob — they have failed to announce it, and for the best of reasons, as not a word nor intimation of such thing is found in the passage. Moreover, those eminent Corporealists, Drs. Jamieson and Fausset, in their comment upon this covenant (Jer. xxxi. 32) say: "The promise to Israel in the last days is effected by an extraordinary outpouring of the Spirit." Good enough! "Out of thine own mouth," etc.

Compare the terms and symbols expressive of

the coming here named, with those before mentioned.

1. Two classes — God's people and their adversaries as in Egypt and in Babylon.

2. The adversaries, powerful and invasive — a peril to Zion.

3. An extraordinary intervention of God by the Spirit and fiery judgments on Egypt and Babylon.

4. The Redeemer came to Zion, and out of Zion to them that turn from their transgressions in Jacob, a fact and form of expression never used of Christ's bodily advent, and which limits this coming to Zion and to repentant sinners in Jacob. Israel's deliverance from Egypt, as also from Babylon, is frequently spoken of as "redemption," and God the Holy One of Israel as their Redeemer. (Ex. vi. 6; 2 Sam. vii. 23; 1 Chron. xvii. 21; Jer. xv. 21; Is. xliv. 23; xlviii. 20; Zech. x. 8.)

5. This coming of the Redeemer and redemption will be according to God's covenant.

"As for me, this is my covenant with them, saith the Lord;
My spirit that is upon thee,
And my words which I have put in thy mouth,

Shall not depart out of thy mouth,
Nor out of the mouth of thy seed,
Nor out of the mouth of thy seed's seed, saith the Lord,
From henceforth and forever." (Is. lix. 21.)

As illustrative of this passage and covenant, Drs. Jamieson, Fausset, and Brown, refer to Christ's command and promise in Matt. xxviii. 19, 20: "Go . . . and lo, I am with you alway, even unto the end of the world." The Writer to the Hebrews at viii. 10 and x. 16 quotes from Jer. xxxi. 33, 34, as fulfilled in his day: —

"But this is the covenant
That I will make with the house of Israel after those days, saith the Lord;
I will put my law in their inward parts,
And in their heart will I write it;
And I will be their God,
And they shall be my people: . . .
And their sin will I remember no more."

God's method of accomplishing the millennial glory, even "righteousness and praise . . . before all the nations," is distinctly declared in this same vision (Is. lxi. 11), of which more in another place.

Again (Zech. xiv 9), is claimed in proof of the

millennial coming of Christ in body. The points of the argument are these: —

1. The passage speaks of a time when the Lord shall be "king over all the earth."

2. Before this (v. 2) all nations "gather against Jerusalem to battle," when "the Lord my God shall come, and all the holy ones." (v. 5.)

3. His feet shall tread upon the Mount of Olives, and the mountain shall divide and its halves remove.

I answer: —

1. This passage is in one of the most symbolical books: horns, carpenters, trees, filling lamps, chariots, mountains of brass, a flying roll, a woman with wings, Judah a bow, Ephraim an arrow, and the Lord the archer, sending His arrows like lightning, blowing His trumpet, encamping about His house, seen coming and going with whirlwinds, returning, visiting, dwelling, defending with sling, storms, hissing, sowing, Lebanon opens its doors to fire, the fir-trees and the oaks howl, Jerusalem is a cup of trembling and a burdensome stone to all people, and the governors of Judah are a torch of fire in a sheaf.

A proof-text from such a book must present unmistakable evidence of its meaning. But such evidence is not at hand, since adventists themselves are not agreed as to its application or meaning. In utter chaos are they when they attempt to work their scheme through the opening verses of the chapter from which this proof-text is taken. For instance, a somewhat noted adventist, D. T. Taylor, in the "World's Crisis," applies the three chapters of Zech. (13–15) to Christ's first advent, and says: "It is surprising that millenarians wrest them by applying them to the second advent."

In order to understand a prophet we must clearly know his time as well as his terms. Haggai and Zechariah were post-exilic prophets, and among the chief builders of the new nation gathered from Babylon after the seventy years' captivity. By Jeremiah God had said that He would visit and restore them after seventy years. Those years had passed, and the first colony under Zerubbabel were rebuilding Jerusalem.

In Zech. i. God says: "Return unto me, and I will return unto you." In ii. 7–13 is God's call to those who still remained in Babylon:—

> "Ho, Zion, escape,
> Thou that dwellest with the daughter of Babylon! . . .
> Sing and rejoice, O daughter of Zion;
> For, lo, I come,
> And will dwell in the midst of thee, saith the Lord. . . .
> Be silent, all flesh, before the Lord:
> For He is waked up out of his Holy habitation."

More distinctly is this last fact set forth in i. 16:—

> "I am returned to Jerusalem with mercies;
> My house shall be built in it."

Also in viii. 3:—

> "I am returned unto Zion, and will dwell in the midst of Jerusalem."

Beyond question is the matter put in x. 3, by the past tense:—

> "The Lord of Hosts hath visited His flock of Judah."

Beyond all possible cavil should the matter be put by the word of God through Hag. ii. 4, 5:—

> . . . "Be strong, O Zerubbabel, saith the Lord;
> And be strong, O Joshua, son of Jehozadak, the high priest;

> And be strong, all ye people of the land, saith the Lord,
>   and work;
> For I am with you, saith the Lord of Hosts,
> According to the word that I covenanted with you
> When ye came out of Egypt,
> *And my spirit abode among you:*
> Fear ye not!"

At Sinai He said: "My presence shall go with thee," and here, a thousand years later, He says to their descendants: "I am with you." "My Spirit abideth (R.V. *marg.*) among you." God promised to come and dwell with the Old Testament saints, and He did so. Hence we read in Ps. xcix. 1:—

> "The Lord reigneth; let the peoples tremble:
>   He sitteth upon the cherubim; let the earth be moved."

Said to have been written with reference to Sennacherib's invasion, Ps. lxxx. 1, 2 reads:—

> "Give ear, O Shepherd of Israel, . . .
>   Thou that sittest upon the cherubim, shine forth.
>   . . . stir up thy might,
>   And come to save us."

In behalf of this imperiled kingdom Hezekiah prayed: "O Lord . . . that sittest upon the cherubim, . . . incline thine ear and hear; open thine eyes and see . . . save us from his hand."

The extreme literalist argues that Zech. xiv. 4, "His feet shall stand upon the Mount of Olives," certainly proves Christ's bodily presence as a man. Why not be consistent and say that this prayer proves that God in the body of a man dwelt between the cherubim, because He is represented as having eyes and ears.

Was it in a human form, a man's body, that God covenanted to dwell with those who came out of Egypt? He who asserts it has it to prove.

But compare the terms of this proof-text with Scripture terms and facts. Zech. xiv. 5: "The Lord my God shall come, and all the holy ones with thee." In Ps. l. 3–5, written a year before the promised coming of the Lord to destroy Babylon and redeem his people; in Is. xiii. 5, Jer. xxix. 10, and Zeph. ii. 7, it is said: —

"Our God shall come . . .
He shall call to the heavens above,
And to the earth, that he may judge His people;
Gather my saints together unto Me;
Those that have made a covenant with Me by sacrifice."

Twenty years later God said by his prophet Zechariah (viii. 3–8) : —

> "I am returned to Zion, and will dwell in the midst of Jerusalem: . . .
> Behold I will save my people from the east country,
> And from the west country;
> And I will bring them, and they shall dwell in the midst of Jerusalem."

There is no mistaking this language. God *had come*, had returned, and was bringing His saints with Him, and those saints were those who had made covenant with Him by sacrifice.

Another example is recorded by Moses (Deut. xxxiii. 1–3) : —

> "The Lord came from Sinai, . . .
> He came from the ten thousands of His holy ones: . . .
> All His saints are in thy hand.
> And they sat down at thy feet;
> Every one shall receive of thy words."

It is said that (Zech. xiv. 4), "His feet shall stand in that day upon the Mount of Olives, and . . . the mount shall cleave in the midst thereof," proves a bodily advent. But it is said by Micah (i. 3, 4) : —

"Behold, the Lord cometh forth out of His place,
  And will come down and tread upon the high places of the earth.
  And the mountains shall be molten under Him,
  And the valleys shall be cleft,
  As wax before the fire, . . .
  For the transgression of Jacob is all this. . . .
  What is the transgression of Jacob? Is it not Samaria? . . .
  Therefore I will make Samaria as a heap of the field."

So in Ps. cxiv. 1–9: —

"When Israel went forth out of Egypt, . . .
  The mountains skipped like rams,
  The little hills like young sheep. . . .
  Tremble thou earth, at the presence of the Lord,
  At the presence of the God of Jacob."

That twice-used word "presence" means literally "face."

Agreeing therewith are the words of God to Moses at Sinai (Ex. iii. 7, 8): "I have seen the affliction of my people which are in Egypt, . . . and am come down to deliver them."

How now did God come down and tread upon the high places of the earth when Samaria was destroyed? Not in body, as a man, but by His appointed agents, the Assyrian army. That which they did by His appointment, He did.

One other verse of this proof-text (Zech. xiv. 3) requires notice: —

> "Then shall the Lord go forth,
> And fight against those nations,
> As when he fought in the day of battle."

As God is said to come and go, it is fair to presume, there being no evidence to the contrary, that the mode of His coming and going is the same. This verse declares that He shall go forth and fight those nations "*as when* He fought in the day of battle." Here is a plain reference to historical examples, and the unequivocal declaration that this will be "as" that. Until the premillennialist points to the historical case in which Christ in body — as a man — went forth and fought His enemies, this passage may be shelved as wholly irrelevant to this argument.

But more than that. This passage in Zechariah is one of the strongest proofs that Christ's millennial coming is, like that, "with power," not bodily. In the Red Sea the Egyptians fled, confessing that

"The Lord fighteth against them." (Ex. xiv. 25.) Moses, in Deut. xx. 4, repeated the same: "The Lord your God is He that goeth with you, to fight for you against your enemies, to save you." And so says Joshua (xxiii. 10): "The Lord your God, He it is that fighteth for you, as He spake unto you," saying, "Cleave unto the Lord your God, as ye have done unto this day." (v. 8.)

Against David's foes the Lord went forth and fought, but by David's own hand (2 Sam. v. 24). By great hailstones he fought Israel's foe (Jos. x. 11); by a raging pestilence against Jerusalem (Jer. xx. 5, 6); by the Medes against Babylon (Is. xiii. 5–17).

Now as Zechariah says that at the time of which he speaks, "The Lord shall go forth and fight against those nations, *as when* He fought in the day of battle," it unmistakably follows that, if this passage refers to the Millennium, Christ's millennial coming will be like those; that is, not in body, but with spiritual power, in extraordinary mercies and judgments. On the other hand, if it does not refer to the Millennium, it has nothing to do with the question before us.

A reign of "a thousand years" is mentioned in Rev. xx. 1-7, the Latin equivalent of which is "millennium," and the Greek, "chiliasm." In the preceding chapter (v. 11) John says: "I saw the heaven opened; and behold, a white horse, and He that sat thereon, called Faithful and True; and in righteousness He doth judge and make war. . . . Out of His mouth proceedeth a sharp sword, that with it He should smite the nations. (v. 15). . . . I saw an angel standing in the sun; and he cried with a loud voice, saying to all the birds that fly in mid heaven: Come and be gathered together unto the great supper of God" (v. 17).

It is claimed and conceded that Rev. xix. 11-21, relates to Christ's conquest of His foes *before* the millennium. It is claimed, but denied, that the appearance of Christ spoken of in the passage is His second bodily advent.

This then is the question. Does this passage speak of Christ's second bodily coming? If Zech. xiv. is a millennial passage, it is a subjective parallel of Rev. xix. and xx. so far as the appearing of Christ and the millennium are concerned.

In both Christ goes forth to battle, and destroys

or subdues His enemies, after which He reigns. But if they are parallels, referring to the same time and event, the mode of Christ's going forth to battle in the one is that of the other. But, as before shown, the mode of His going forth in past history was judicial, not bodily. As was the mode to Zechariah, so must it be to John, — if they are parallels.

In both He appears as a man of war; goes forth to battle; and triumphs. In both the result of His triumph is His actual reign in all the earth.

Now His appearing in Zech. xiv. 3, is as when He went out "to smite the host of the Philistines" (1 Chron. xiv. 14, 15); the Egyptians (Ex. xiv. 14–25); the Canaanites (Jos. xxiii. 3–10); the Assyrians (2 Kings xix. 35); and the Babylonians (Is. xiii. 5).

But His second descent from heaven will be as He went up into heaven: "This Jesus, . . . shall so come in like manner as ye beheld Him going into heaven" (Acts i. 11). But the appearing in Rev. xix. is nothing like His ascension, nor can its symbols be interpreted literally, without the most monstrous absurdities. The material man Jesus, sitting on a material horse, with a material sword coming out of His mouth, with which He slays His enemies, is grotesque absurdity itself.

In order to escape this the Corporealists mix things, and assume a material Christ sitting or a symbolic horse with a symbolic sword. The logical result of that can only be a " symbolic " destruction of His enemies, which cannot hurt them much.

How much better by far to allow the prophets to explain each other, and to interpret this passage from the most symbolic book of the Bible as other passages are explained, and according to its evident meaning, as setting forth in symbols, after the manner of all the prophets, the judicial appearance of Christ; as when in all ages of the church He has gone forth to terrible things for the redemption of His people by His Spirit and by judgments upon His foes.

Abounds the Old Testament with symbolic passages similar to this. For example, Hab. iii. 1-15: —

"God came from Teman, . . .
His glory covered the heavens,
And the earth was full of His praise. . . .

> He stood, and measured the earth;
> He beheld, and drove asunder the nations:
> And the eternal mountains were scattered,
> The everlasting hills did bow. . . .
> . . . Thou didst ride upon Thy horses,
> Upon Thy chariots of salvation. . . .
> Thou didst march through the land in indignation,
> Thou didst thresh the nations in anger.
> Thou wentest forth for the salvation of Thy people. . . .
> Thou didst tread the sea with Thine horses,
> The heap of mighty waters."

This is history presented in the highly emotional dress of poetry. More than two-fifths of the Old Testament is poetry, and is to be judged by nothing but poetical canons. This passage is but the poetical review and expansion of Moses' description of God's march from Sinai (Deut. xxxiii. 1–3):—

> "The Lord came from Sinai,
> And rose from Seir unto them;
> He shined forth from Paran,
> And He came from the ten thousands of holy ones:
> At His right hand was a fiery law unto them.
> Yea, He loveth the peoples:
> All His saints are in Thy hand.
> And they sat down at Thy feet;
> Every one shall receive of Thy words."

"Receiving His words," is the cold prose for "sitting at His feet" as pupils, its poetical form. No sane man would interpret these descriptions as teaching a bodily coming, marching, walking, riding upon horses, and a physical scattering of the mountains. Why then do men interpret these very same symbols in the most symbolic of the biblical books as denoting the bodily coming of Christ? Why is this done, in direct contradiction of prophets and angels?

The prophet Zechariah (xiv. 3), said: —

"Then shall the Lord go forth,
And fight against those nations,
As when He fought in the day of battle."

We have seen how that was, — that it was not by bodily presence and going, but judicial. And as millennial is the passage claimed by the Corporealists.

Again, the angels in Acts i. 11, not only announce the fact of Christ's second advent, but also the manner of it: "This Jesus . . . shall so come in like manner as ye beheld him going into heaven." Is that the manner of His appearing in Rev. xix.

11? Did they see Him riding up into heaven on a horse? followed by an army upon horses? If not, then the appearing in Rev. xix. 11 is not the second coming of Christ promised by the angels in Acts i. 11.

So much for history and its light upon Christ's millennial coming. We have examined the texts which speak both of the coming of the Lord Christ and the millennium, and have found not one that teaches a premillennial bodily coming. Rather have we found decidedly the opposite, viz.: that His millennial coming, like others in sacred history, is a judicial one, in extraordinary mercies and judgments.

This is the direct, positive testimony of the Scriptures. What men may infer from presuppositions and assumptions from wrested texts, dove-tailed to suit a theory, is of little consequence, in the presence of inspired testimony as to the manner of the Millennial Coming, when in doing terrible things in righteousness He comes down, and the mountains of difficulties and peril shall melt at His glorious though invisible presence.

EVEN SO, COME, LORD JESUS.

III. THE WORLD'S CONVERSION AFTER CHRIST'S SECOND ADVENT IMPOSSIBLE.

By the predicted conversion of the world is meant the reconstruction of human society upon the Scriptural basis: "One is your master, The Christ; and all ye are brethren." The result is to be peace and prosperity, universal and final. It is to be an era in which Christ will be *de facto*, as long *de jure*, the Sovereign of the world, while His redemptive agencies will achieve their grandest triumphs in the salvation of men from sin to holiness.

Such state of affairs is the Millennium of Scripture, a condition of mortality, of probation, and of the utmost activity of the powers of Christ's Kingdom. Christ's second advent is his return in body from heaven. This return from heaven in a real body, distinguishes said coming from many of the former comings.

Our argument is that the conditions essential to the Scriptural millennium cease and terminate at Christ's second advent, and that hence there can be no such millennium thereafter. For brevity I use the word millennium as the synonym of the phrase, "the world's conversion."

Here is the first argument: —

1. The millennium is a condition or state of mortality.

2. But mortality ends at Christ's second advent.

3. Therefore there can be no millennium after said advent.

All admit the first proposition, viz.: the millennium is a state of mortality. The second, that mortality ends at Christ's second advent is proven by two facts. 1. All that are Christ's put on immortality at Christ's second advent. 2. At that time — "then" — Death is abolished, after which there can be no mortality.

Christ declared it to be His Father's will "that of all that which He hath given me I should lose nothing, but should raise it up at the last day." Paul repeats this and locates it definitely: "They that are Christ's at His coming" (1 Cor. xv. 23). Again (1 Thess. iv. 16–18), "The Lord himself shall descend from heaven . . . and the dead in Christ shall rise first; then we that are alive, that are left, shall together with them be caught up in the clouds, to meet the Lord in the air; and so shall we be ever with the Lord."

Again, Christ and Paul teach that the righteous will be changed to immortality instantly and simultaneously. At His voice shall come forth "they that have done good, unto the resurrection of life" (John v. 29). "We shall not all sleep," says Paul (1 Cor. xv. 51, 52), "but we shall all be changed, in a moment, in the twinkling of an eye." The fact then that all that the Father hath given to Christ will put on immortality instantly and simultaneously, is here declared as plainly as words can declare anything.

Already have we quoted the declaration that these changes will be when the Lord himself descends from heaven. Death will be abolished when the saints put on immortality, *i. e.*, at Christ's second advent. Isaiah said that God will swallow up death in victory. Paul (1 Cor. xv. 53, 54) quotes this saying, and tells us when Christ's saints put on immortality. Of the righteous he says: "This mortal must put on immortality. But when . . . this mortal shall have put on immortality, then shall come to pass the saying that is written,

'Death is swallowed up in victory,'" *i. e.*, shall be completely abolished.

Now Paul had said that there shall be a resurrection of the just and the unjust. Christ had said: "All that are in the tombs shall hear his voice, and shall come forth;" incontestibly at the same moment and command. And here Paul declares that mortality shall be absolutely abolished when the righteous put on immortality at the second advent of Christ.

His terms "when" and "then" according to their meaning and use are shut up to this conclusion. The first and fullest meaning of the word rendered "when," is whenever (See Strong's or Young's Conc.), and this is its chief New Testament usage. The original for "then" has but one meaning, viz.: *at that time*. Paul used it eighteen times, and this is its only meaning with his. In its one hundred and sixty occurrences in the New Testament, it has but this one meaning.

In the passage considered, Paul's meaning is unquestionably this: that whenever the righteous put on immortality, then — at that time — death will be abolished by the resurrection of the wicked,

WORLD'S CONVERSION IMPOSSIBLE. 331

for death cannot be abolished till the entire race is raised or changed.

But since it is proved, and all admit, that all the righteous will put on immortality at Christ's second advent, and since the Millennium is confessedly a condition of mortality, and since that condition ceases at Christ's second advent, there can be no millennium after that advent.

Confirmed is this view by the Church Father, Justin Martyr, an eminent Premillennialist, though not of the modern sort, in the following words: —

"Christ . . . became incarnate . . . in order that . . . the serpent that sinned . . . may be destroyed, and that death may forever quit at the second coming of Christ himself . . . and be no more, when some are sent to be punished unceasingly . . . but others shall exist in freedom from suffering in immortality." (Ante-Nicene Lib., vol. 2, p. 144. Edinburgh Ed. 1870.)

It having been shown that Christ's second advent ends mortality, it will next be set forth that it also ends probation by the universal eternal judgment.

Paul's quotation above is from Is. xlv. 23–25: —

> "By myself have I sworn,
>> The word is gone forth from my mouth in righteousness,
>> And shall not return,
>> That unto me every knee shall bow,
>> Every tongue shall swear.
>> Only in the Lord, shall one say unto me,
>> Is righteousness and strength;
>> Even to Him shall men come,
>> And all they that were incensed against Him shall be ashamed.
>> In the Lord shall all the seed of Israel be justified,
>> And shall glory."

Notice the universality, "men;" "all they that were incensed against him;" "all the seed of Israel;" all the righteous and all the wicked. Where? Paul answers — "At the judgment of Christ." When? "After death." And then, as if Paul foresaw the modern perversion of this "death," he applies it to all Christians as a part of the "men;" "we shall all stand before the judgment seat of God." Each one of us shall — not only be there but — give an account of himself to God.

One judgment, universal in its subjects and eternal in its allotments, was the teaching of Christ and his apostles. This is called "the judgment," "the day of judgment," and is explained by Paul as that day, in which God will judge the inhabited earth . . . in the man whom he hath ordained" (Acts xvii. 31).

That the universality of this judgment included saints and sinners, is declared by Paul and proved from the Old Testament in these words, addressed to the Christians at Rome: "we shall all stand before the judgment seat of God. For it is written:—

'As I live, saith the Lord, to me shall every knee bow,
And every tongue shall confess to God.'

So then each one of us shall give an account of himself to God" (Rom. xiv. 10–12).

The universality and simultaneousness of the judgment at His second advent did Christ unquestionably declare in the parable of the wheat and the tares. Therein both wheat and tares are gathered each and all to their final destiny at one and the same time. Likewise in the parable of the net, the good were gathered and the evil cast away at one and the same time, and both at the end of the same age.

Similarly in the parable of the pounds, when the nobleman returned, the first called to give account of themselves were the servants, then the citizens, and, in direct terms apart from parable, Christ said (Matt. xvi. 27): "The Son of Man shall come in the glory of His Father with His angels; and *then* shall He render unto every man according to his deeds." And in His description of this coming and judgment (Matt. xxv. 31–46) He announces the final allotments of both the righteous and the wicked, eternal life to the one, and eternal punishment to the other.

Paul's words respecting this judgment at the second advent of Christ put beyond all cavil the simultaneousness of the judgment of all men at Christ's advent. "It is a righteous thing with God to recompense affliction to them that afflict you, and to you that are afflicted rest with us, at the revelation of the Lord Jesus from heaven with the angels of His power."

Then, as if he foresaw some notions now prevalent, Paul notably proceeds: " . . . rendering vengeance to them that knew not God, and to them that obey not the Gospel of our Lord Jesus; who shall suffer punishment, even eternal destruction from the face of the Lord and from the glory of His might, when He shall come to be glorified in His saints" (2 Thess. i. 6–10).

As to this passage notice:—

1. That it speaks of Christ's second advent, *i. e.*, of His revelation from heaven with His mighty angels to be glorified in His saints.

2. That the recompense of the righteous and of the wicked are at the same time, *i. e.*, when He shall come to be glorified in His saints, *i. e.*, at His second advent.

3. That this assignment of both the righteous and the wicked to their final destiny implies their judgment, which Christ says will be at His coming in His Father's glory, or His second advent.

4. That this universal and eternal judgment ends probation. But the Scriptural millennium is a condition of probation. Therefore as probation ends at the Judgment, which will be at the second advent and will include all men everywhere, there can be no millennium after Christ's second advent.

5. That at Christ's second advent the righteous and wicked are separated absolutely and forever. But during the millennium of the Scriptures the righteous and the wicked are together. Hence the millennium of the Scriptures cannot be after Christ's second advent.

That the righteous and the wicked are absolutely and forever parted at Christ's second advent, is implied and proven by the fact already considered, viz.: the judgment of all men everywhere at His second coming. The parable of the wheat and the tares puts this matter beyond dispute. Both are to grow together until the harvest, and the harvest is the end of the age, and the reapers are the angels. As the tares are gathered together and burned in the fire, so shall it be in the end of this age.

The Son of Man shall send forth His angels and they shall gather out of His kingdom all things that offend and them that do iniquity, and shall cast them into the furnace of fire. Then — at that time — shall the righteous shine in the kingdom of their Father. And as if Christ foresaw the perversity of error, to stop it, He repeats the same truth in the parable of the net, in which were gathered of every kind, and being filled it was drawn to the shore, and the good gathered into vessels, and the bad cast away. "So it shall be," says Christ, "at the end of the age. The angels shall come forth and shall sever the wicked from among the just, and shall cast them into the furnace of fire."

All parties admit what the texts abundantly prove, that the age spoken of in these parables is the Gospel age or dispensation. Now it is not a matter of opinion or interpretation, but of unequivocal declaration: —

1. That during this age, until the harvest tares are "among" the wheat, *i. e.*, the wicked are among the just; but

2. That in the harvest, which is the gathering of the whole crop, the tares, the wicked, are severed from among the just, and each assigned their final destiny.

3. That this absolute severance of the wicked from among the just is at the Judgment, when Christ shall come in the glory of His Father with His angels at the end of this age or dispensation. Now, after this final assignment of eternal life to the just and eternal punishment to the wicked at

Christ's second advent, — after this gathering of the entire race to their eternal state, who will be converted? Not the just in heaven, not the wicked in hell. What then is the material for conversion after Christ's second advent, and whence comes it?

4. The conversion of the world or the Scriptural millennium is Christ's triumph, as King of Kings. But He delivers up His Kingdom at His second coming. Therefore there can be no millennium after that advent.

The first of these just named postulates is admitted, and needs no argument. The millennium is that condition of the world in which "All kings shall fall down before Him and all nations shall serve Him" (Ps. lxxii. 11).

The second of them is declared by Paul who, with extraordinary precision, has shown the beginning and the close of Christ's reign. For its beginning: "He raised Him from the dead, and made Him to sit at His right hand in the heavenly places, far above all rule, and authority, and power, and dominion, and every name that is named, . . . and He put all things in subjection under His feet" (Eph. i. 20–22).

WORLD'S CONVERSION IMPOSSIBLE. 339

The close of this reign is declared in the decree: "Sit thou at My right hand, until I make thine enemies thy footstool" (Ps. cx. 1).

Explicitly does Paul declare that all the race shall be made alive by Christ — every man in his own company, "they that are His at His coming," — and then is the end, when He shall deliver up the kingdom to God the Father, when He shall have put down all rule and authority and power, for He must reign till He hath put all enemies under His feet, even the last which is death. Here Paul says that Christ will deliver up His Kingdom when He has abolished death. The abolition of death is His last redemptive act. But, as shown before by Paul's direct testimony, Christ will abolish death at His second advent. Therefore there can be no millennium or conversion of the world after that advent.

That this view is correct is proven by the fact that the redemptive powers and agencies of Christ's kingdom cease as such at Christ's second advent.

The time of Christ's redemptive work is called by Isaiah "a day of salvation" (xlix. 1–8). Thus saith the Lord — to Christ: —

"I will also give Thee for a light to the Gentiles,
That thou mayest be my salvation unto the end of the
earth.

. . . .

In an acceptable time I have answered thee,
And in a day of salvation have I helped thee,
And I will preserve thee, and give thee for a covenant of the people."

In the next eighteen verses Isaiah describes the triumph of Christ's reign in the day of salvation mentioned in verses 6–8. In chapter ii. 2–4 the same prophet says that that triumph will be an era of peace on earth, so that the nations will learn war no more. This is the conversion of the world, or millennium of the Scriptures. And the prophet says this shall come to pass in the last days (chap. ii. 2).

Now Peter and Paul expressly declare that the last days had begun in their time. "God . . . hath at the end of these days spoken unto us in His son" (Heb. i. 1). This is that which hath been spoken by the prophet Joel:—

"And it shall be in the last days, saith God,
I will pour forth of my Spirit upon all flesh" (Acts ii. 16, 17).

And Paul (2 Cor. vi. 2) quotes Isaiah's words as fulfilled at the moment of his writing: "Behold, now is the acceptable time; behold, now is the day of salvation."

All parties agree that Paul speaks of the Gospel dispensation or age called "the last days." And as Isaiah says that the era of universal and final peace shall come "in the last days," it follows as a matter of direct revelation, that the conversion of the world will be in the present age or dispensation, and not in another after the advent. Again, the last days will close with the last day, and as the last day is the day of resurrection and the eternal judgment at Christ's second advent, and as it is the last of the periods to end, there can be no day of salvation after it.

Thus the redemptive powers and agencies of Christ's kingdom cease as such at His second advent. Christ's mediatorial work must cease when He takes the throne of eternal judgment at His coming. And Paul says that He shall appear the second time without sin. The word "sin" in this connection cannot mean guilt, for Christ never knew guilt. "The same Hebrew word," says Dr.

Steele, "is used in the Old Testament one hundred and sixty times for sin, and one hundred and twelve times for sin-offering. Paul evidently uses the equivalent Greek word in the sense of sin-offering, or in his own words, "sacrifice for sin." Thus if we understand Paul to mean that Christ's atonement ceases to atone for sin at His second appearing, our conclusion harmonizes with the other teachings of Paul and Christ.

As before seen Paul teaches that the righteous and the wicked will receive their eternal awards when Christ shall be revealed from heaven to be glorified in His saints. And Christ himself limits the saving power of His kingdom by His coming: "Occupy till I come." "As often as ye eat this bread, and drink the cup, ye proclaim the Lord's death till he come" (1 Cor. x. 26). "The bridegroom came; and they that were ready went in . . . and the door was shut" (Matt. xxv. 10). "Go ye therefore, and make disciples of all the nations, . . . and lo, I am with you alway, even unto the end of the aion,"— age. (Matt. xxviii. 19–20).

How was Christ to be with His evangelizing church? Plainly by the Holy Spirit. How long?

WORLD'S CONVERSION IMPOSSIBLE. 343

Unto the end of the age. When does that age end? At Christ's second advent. A millennium without Christ's mediation and atonement; without the Holy Spirit as the executive of the Godhead and the regenerator and sanctifier, and a church divinely commissioned and empowered; may exist in the imagination of erring men. But never the millennium of the Scripture.

Finally. At Christ's second coming the earth will be so dissolved by fire as to disappear forever. Therefore a millennium of converted nations upon it after that advent is impossible. Paul speaks of "the revelation of the Lord Jesus from heaven . . . in flaming fire . . . when He shall come to be glorified in His saints" (1 Thess. i. 8-10). In exposing the scoffers who deny His coming, Peter declares that: "The heavens that now are, and the earth, by the same word have been stored up for fire, being reserved against the day of judgment and destruction of ungodly men" (2 Peter iii. 7). "The day of the Lord" — of His advent — "will come . . . in the which the heavens shall pass away with a great noise, and the elements shall be dissolved with fervent heat, and the earth and the works that are therein shall be burned up" (2 Peter iii. 10).

In describing that judgment, John says: "I saw a great white throne, and him that sat upon it, from whose face the earth and the heaven fled away; and there was found no place for them" (Rev. xx. 11). Following this is the most minute description of the resurrection and judgment to be found in the Bible. In the next chapter, John repeats as follows: "The first heaven and the first earth are passed away" (xxi. 1).

By this repetition John emphasizes the fact that our heaven and earth are to depart from their place, and when he adds "there was found no place for them," this statement must be accepted, and not ignored as is strangely done by every theory of renovation and reconstruction of the old heavens and earth. Decisive are Peter's words, when he says that at the day of judgment — the day of the Lord's coming, — not only that the earth and its work shall be burned, dissolved, but its constituent elements, as the word means, "shall melt with fervent heat," and this he repeats.

And when John adds: "They fled away and no

WORLD'S CONVERSION IMPOSSIBLE. 345

place was found for them," he asserts not only what will be, but what has been with other worlds which have disappeared from their place in the heavens. There will be a new heaven and earth, but as John says, these will be AFTER, NOT DURING, the millennium.

Our argument here is this: —

1. Paul, Peter, and John in these texts speak of Christ's second advent — not a third, but the second.

2. At that advent our earth is to disappear forever.

3. Therefore a millennium of converting and converted men upon it after that advent is an impossibility.

The various conflicting and rejected devices to relieve premillennialism from the destructive force of these passages, show plainly its desperate condition. Some would limit the conflagration to old Rome; others to Papal Rome; others to Europe.

But the most popular device is the assumption that the day of the Lord may be, and therefore will be, a thousand years, and that it may be, and therefore will be that Christ will come at the beginning of the thousand years and will burn the world at its close with the millennium between.

This makes Peter and Paul false witnesses, for they unquestionably place the conflagration at Christ's coming, and Paul distinctly says that Christ's revelation in flaming fire and the eternal destruction of the wicked will be "when He comes to be glorified in His saints." Not a thousand years after.

Again this device is demolished by Christ's parable of the nobleman, who judged the servants and citizens on his return and at the same time, — also His parable of the wheat and tares, and the net. In each of these, final allotments are made at one and the same time, — at the end of the age, or at the second advent, not a thousand years after.

That which Paul implies and Peter declares, John describes, — Christ on the throne of eternal judgment, before whose face the heaven and the earth flee away, so that no place was found for them; the resurrection of the dead, small and great, and their judgment, and then the new heaven and the new earth, wherein dwelleth righteousness only.

Some have an easy way of assuming that what they wish will be, because for aught they know it may be. Thus an Essayist at the Prophetic Conference solved the problem of finding population for the millennial earth after the burning of our earth, by boldly asserting that a remnant of men in the flesh will escape the consuming fire described by Peter. But in view of the terms used by Peter, it is doubtful if he would take the chances.

Thus have we glanced at the testimony of Christ and His Apostles respecting these several points, viz.: Christ's second advent will end mortality, probation, the mixture of good and evil, His mediatorial kingdom, His commission to the Church, the redemptive work of the Holy Spirit, and the earth itself. If either of these postulates is true, the hope of the conversion of the world, or any part of it, after that advent, IS A DREAM.

ANTINOMIANISM CHARACTERIZED.

By the Rev. Robert Hall, D. D.

Long time Pastor of the Baptist Church in Bristol, Eng.

"Pray, sir," asked Robert Hall of a Scotch pastor, "have you got any Antinomians in Scotland?"

"None," was the reply, "who avow themselves such. There are individuals in our congregations who have what I consider a morbid aversion to practical preaching, and to minute enforcement of duty; but almost all our people who know and care anything about religion will tell you that although the believer is delivered from the law as a covenant of works, he is subject to it as a rule of life."

"That," said Mr. Hall, "is precisely what I expected. Your ministers and your people have too much information to be ensnared by such im-

ANTINOMIANISM CHARACTERIZED. 349

pieties. Antinomianism is a monster which can live only in darkness; bring light on it, and it expires."

HALL'S WORKS, *Harper's ed., vol. iii., p. 78.*

"THE author is at a loss to conceive on what principle, or for what reason, dangerous concessions are due to antinomianism; that thick-skinned monster of the ooze and the mire, which no weapon can pierce, no discipline can tame. . . . While antinomianism is making such rapid strides through the land, and has already convulsed and disorganized so many of our churches, it is no season for half measures; danger is to be repelled by intrepid resistance, by stern defiance, not by compliances and concessions." . . .

HALL'S WORKS, *Harper's ed., vol. i., p. 390.*

"As almost every age of the church is marked by its appropriate visitation of error, so little penetration is requisite to perceive that antinomianism is the epidemic malady of the present, and that it is an evil of gigantic size and deadly malignity. It is qualified for mischief by the very properties which might seem to render it merely an object of contempt, — its vulgarity of conception, its paucity of ideas, its determined hostility to taste, science, and letters. It includes, within a compass which every head can contain and every tongue can utter, a system which cancels every moral tie, consigns the whole human race to the extremes of presumption or despair, erects religion on the ruins of morality, and imparts to the dregs of stupidity all the powers of the most active poison. The author will ever feel himself honored by whatever censures he may incur through his determined opposition to such a system."

HALL'S WORKS, *Harper's ed., vol. i., p. 390.*

"WE may conceive of a religious code under all the possible gradations of laxness or severity — of its demanding more or less, or of its enforcing its injunctions by penalties more or less formidable; but to form a conception of a system deserving the name of religion, which prescribes no duties whatever, and is enforced by no sanctions, seems an impossibility.

On this account it appears to me improper to speak of antinomianism as a *religious* error; religion, whether true or false, has nothing to do with it; it is rather to be considered as an attempt to substitute a system of subtle and specious impiety in the room of Christianity.

In its own estimation, its disciples are a privileged class, who dwell in a secluded region of unshaken security and lawless liberty, while the rest of the Christian world are the vassals of legal bondage, toiling in darkness and chains. Hence, whatever diversity of character they may display in other respects, a haughty and bitter disdain of every other class of professors is a universal feature. Contempt or hatred of the most devout and enlightened Christians out of their own pale seems one of the most essential elements of their being; nor were the ancient Pharisees ever more notorious for trusting in themselves that they were righteous and despising others." . . .

"The only attempt they make to support their miserable system is to adduce a number of detached and insulated passages of Scripture, forcibly torn from their context, and interpreted with more regard to their sound than their meaning, as ascertained by the laws of sober criticism." . . .

"The most effectual antidote to the leaven of antinomianism will probably be in the frequent and earnest inculcation of the practical precepts of the gospel; in an accurate delineation of the Christian temper; in a specific and minute exposition of the personal, social, and relative duties, enforced at one time by the endearing, at another by the alarming, motives which revelation abundantly suggests."

> HALL'S WORKS, *Preface to Chase's "Antinomianism Unmasked," Harper's ed., vol. ii., pp. 458-461.*

SIN "IN" US BUT NOT "ON" US.

This play on words, to which reference was made on page 105, is aptly illustrated by the utterance of the late Dr. James H. Brooks of St. Louis, editor of *The Truth*. In the issue of July, 1895, his answer to a subscriber is a sample of the interpretation of the Bible which is current among the Plymouth Brethren and their sympathizers of whatever name. The last sentence gives the doctrine in a nutshell.

"Probably it is a new subscriber to *The Truth* who writes to ask: 'What are your views on Sal-

ANTINOMIANISM CHARACTERIZED. 353

vation from Sin?' The editor has no views at all, which would be of any value, but tries to give the views of God, which are of infinite importance.

"'The blood of Jesus Christ, His Son, cleanseth us from all sin' (1 John i. 7);

"'Christ died for our sins according to the Scriptures' (1 Cor. xv. 3);

"'Who His own self bare our sins in His own body on the tree' (1 Pet. ii. 24).

"So the Bible from first to last assures us that Christ has redeemed His people from the penalty, the power, and dominion of sin. But the Bible is equally explicit in testifying that 'there is not a just man upon earth, that doeth good, and sinneth not' (Eccl. vii. 20); 'if we,' that is, we believers, 'say that we have no sin, we deceive ourselves, and the truth is not in us' (1 John i. 81).

"In other words, we have no sin *on* us, thank God; but we have sin *in* us, and will have to the end of the journey."

How absent is perspective from this method of interpreting the Holy Scripture! Were the phrase from Ecclesiastes God's view *before* Christ came, what evidence is there that it was his view *after* the completion of Christ's saving work? But more than that, is the divinely recorded sigh of the pessimist in Ecclesiastes to be understood as the thought of God? And in the case of 1 John it is just as allowable and as much the "view of God" to insert after, "if we," that is, all we who by birth belong to a sinful race, etc.

JOHN WESLEY once described antinomianism as a putting of "Gospel heads on bodies ready to indulge every unholy temper." (WORKS, *Am. ed., vol. vi., p. 779.*)

Wesleyan is the following, on James ii. 26.

> "Dreamers of your salvation sure,
>   Awaking unto righteousness,
> Your Antinomian faith abjure,
>   Your groundless hope, and hellish peace;
> Arise, and wash away your sins;
> And then — the work of faith begins!"
>   POETICAL WORKS, *vol. xiii., p. 172.*

Note to Page 100.

While journeying into New England, Jesse Lee copied from a tombstone in Danbury, Conn., the following: —

"Here lies until the resurrection, the body of Robert Sandeman, a native of Perth, North Britain, who, in the face of continual opposition from all sorts of men, long and boldly contended for the ancient faith; that the bare work of Jesus Christ without a deed, or a thought, on the part of man, is sufficient to present the chief of sinners, spotless before God." ("Life of Jesse Lee," p. 218.)

The cry of this man and his followers was, "A bare faith in a bare Christ!"

Note to Page 165.

A handful of Americans, fragments of families, possessed by this infantile interpretation of Scripture, are eking out an existence in Jerusalem. They have adopted and are called by the name of "The American Colony." They are determined to be at the head of the line of office-seekers when the new administration comes in. The Editor of the *Christian Advocate* has severely characterized this colony.

INDEX TO SCRIPTURAL PASSAGES.

Chap.	Verse.	Page.
GENESIS.—		
XV.	11	18
XVII.	8	122
EXODUS.—		
III.	7, 8	318
VI.	6	310
XIV.	14–25	322
	19–25	287
	25	320
XXIX.	42–46	286
LEVITICUS.—		
IX.	4–6	287
XXIII.	16, 17	73
NUMBERS.—		
XIV.	12	71
	22, 23	71
XXIII.	21	70
	21	145
XXV.	1	146
DEUTERONOMY.—		
XX.	4	320
XXXIII.	1–3, 317	324
JOSHUA.—		
X.	11	320
XXIII.	3–10	322
	3–10	320
2 SAMUEL.—		
V.	24	320
VII.	23	310
XXII.	10–18	303
2 KINGS.—		
XIX.	35	322
1 CHRONICLES.—		
XIV.	9–17	289
	14, 15	322
XVII.	21	310
PSALMS.—		
XI.	6	306
XLVI.		293
L.	3–5	296, 316
LI.		70
LXXII.		304
	5	307
	9	307
	11	338
LXXX.	1, 2	315
XCVII.	1–5	287
XCIX.	1	315
CII.	13	296
CX.	1	339
CXIV.	1–9	318

INDEX TO SCRIPTURAL PASSAGES.

Chap.	Verse.	Page.
ISAIAH.—		
I.	27	294
II.	4	227
	24	340
IX.	6, 8	227
XIII.	1, 5	299
	5	316, 322
	5–17	320
	17	300
	19	300
XIV.	1, 2	191
XXIV.	5	133
XXXIV.	1–6	303
XXXVII.	16, 17	315
	35, 36	292
XLIV.	3, 4	305
	23	310
XLV.	23–25	351f
XLVIII.	20	310
XLIX.	1–6	339f
	9–27	340
LVII.	15	286
LIX.	16–LXIII. 12, 307f
	21	309ff
LXI.	11	311
LXIII.	17	291
LXIV.	1–3	291
	3	288
LXV.	21	228
	23	227
JEREMIAH.—		
XII.	7	294
XIV.	10–12	295
XV.	21	310
XVII.	10	29
XX.	5, 6	320

Chap.	Verse.	Page.
JEREMIAH—Continued.		
XXIII.	39	294
XXIV.	1–7	295
XXV.	26	300
XXIX.	10	316
	10–13	296
XXXI.	31–34	309
	33, 34	311
XXXII.	19	29
L.	31, 32	299
EZEKIEL.—		
VII.	3, 27	29
XVIII.	20, 30	29
XXXIV.	26	305
XXXVI.	26	24
XXXVIII.		284
	21–23	303f
HOSEA.—		
V.	14, 15	289
VI.	3	305
XII.	10	284
XIV.	5	305
JOEL.—		
II.	28–32	212, 340
AMOS.—		
IV.	12	289
V.	7	289
MICAH.—		
I.	3, 4	317f
	3–6	289
HABAKKUK.—		
III.	1–15	323f
ZEPHANIAH.—		
II.	7	316

INDEX TO SCRIPTURAL PASSAGES.

Chap.	Verse.	Page.
HAGGAI.—		
II.	4, 5	314
	15	298
	21, 22	299
ZECHARIAH.—		
I.		313
	16	314
	16, 17	297
II.	6–10	297
	7–13	313f
VIII.	3	297f, 314
	3–8	317
	4, 5	228
X.	3	314
	8	310
XIII.–XV.		313
XIV.		204ff, 321
	2–5	312
	3	320, 322, 325
	4	316f
	5	316
	9	311
	21	190–192
MALACHI.—		
III.	1–5	300
MATTHEW.—		
V.	22	72
VII.	27	307
XIII.	31–33	171
XVI.	27	334
	28	275
XVIII.	20	12
XIX.	28	256
	29	276
XXV.	9	276
	10	342

Chap.	Verse.	Page.
MATTHEW XXV — Continued.		
	32–46	29, 167, 190–192, 226, 228, 264, 275, 334
XXVIII.	19	166, 277
	19, 20	311, 342
MARK.—		
I.	15	275
IX.	1	275f
X.	30	302
XVI.	15	277
LUKE.—		
I.	74, 75	61
XVII.	21	276
XXII.	28–30	257
	30	277
JOHN.—		
III.	6	114
	16, 17	264
	18	178
V.	24	87, 132, 179
	25 ff	236
	29	229
VI.	47	132
	54	118
XII.	47	264
XIII.		81
XIV.	23	286
XV.	1–7	157
ACTS.—		
I.	6	275f
	11	322, 325
II.	16	340
	17	213
III.	21	260
X.	34	175
	42	229
XVII.	31	333
XXVIII.	23	276

INDEX TO SCRIPTURAL PASSAGES.

Chap.	Verse.	Page.
ROMANS.—		
II.	6–16	175
III.	8	38
VI.	1	31, 38
	7	61
	11, R.V.	159
	19, 22	61
	25, R.V.	159
VII.	6	109
VIII.	1	177
	2	159
	3	123
	33–39	159, 178
X.	9	104
XI.	25	256
	26, 27	309
XIV.	10–12	153, 333
XVI.	2, 7, 10	156
1 CORINTHIANS.—		
I.	2	155
	4, R.V.	159
	30	155
III.	8, 13–15	29
VII.	39	156
IX.	21	109
X.	26	342
XV.	3	353
	18	154
	23, 24	264
	23	326
	51–54	329
2 CORINTHIANS.—		
V.	10	29, 184
	17	156
	19	159
	21	125
VI.	2	341

Chap.	Verse.	Page.
2 COR. VI.—Continued.		
	18	107
VII.	1	107
	2	61
XII.		146
GALATIANS.—		
I.	6	84
II.	4	159
	17	119
	20	25
III.	5	84
	13	178
	14, R.V.	159
V.	17	84
VI.	5–8	29
EPHESIANS.—		
I.	3	159
II.	4	155
	19, 20	86, 179
	20–22	336
	6, 7, R.V.	159
III.	11	159
IV.	21	154
	32, R.V.	159
V.	6	38
	20, R.V.	72, 156
PHILIPPIANS.—		
II.	5	159
III.	10, 11	239
COLOSSIANS.—		
II.	11, R.V.	61
1 THESSALONIANS.—		
I.	8–10	343
III.	13	61

INDEX TO SCRIPTURAL PASSAGES. 361

Chap.	Verse.	Page.
1 THESS. — *Continued.*		
IV.	7	61
	15–17	276
	16, 17	163
	16–18	328
2 THESSALONIANS. —		
I.	6–10	264, 334f
II.	10	61
2 TIMOTHY. —		
II.	10	159
IV.	10	61
HEBREWS. —		
I.	1	340
III.	6, 14	180
VI.	1, R.V.	101
VIII.	1–13	309
	10	211
IX.	27	184
X.	10	155
	15–17	309
	16	211
XII.	10, 14, 23	61
XIII.	11	126
JAMES. —		
II.	17–26	38
	20	113
IV.	4–6, R.V.	75
1 PETER. —		
II.	24	353
III.	16	154
	18	103
IV.	5	229
V.	14	154

Chap.	Verse.	Page.
2 PETER. —		
I.	10, 11	106
II.	18, 19	38
III.		263
	7–10	343f
1 JOHN. —		
I.	7–9	106, 353
	8–10	82
II.	18	276
III.	9	64–68
IV.	17	61
V.	19, R.V.	160
3 JOHN. —		
	9–10	57
REVELATION. —		
III.	20	286
X.	7	275
XIV.	13	154
XIX.		322
XIX–XX.		321
XIX.	11	325f
	11–21	321
XX.		237–245
	1–7	321
	1–11	273ff
	7–9	198
	11	227, 344
	11–15	163, 229
XXI.	1	344
XXII.	11–15	274
	14, R.V.	180

INDEX TO SUBJECTS AND NAMES.

(Leading subjects are quite fully analyzed. A topic not found under one, may be sought for under another.)

Page.

Alford,
  Living commensurate
    with believing . . . 88
  On Regeneration 116
  Opposes some Prem. arguments 249
"American Colony" at
  Jerusalem 355
Anderson, Robt. (commended by Moody).
  Minifies Repentance . . 97
Antinomian-ism.
  Absurdities of 107
  Abuse of figurative language 133
  Abuse of "Texts" . . 351-3
  Agricola well expressed . 46-7
  Antidote to 352
  Augsburg Confession on . 46
  Based on "Election" . . 48
  Baxter opposed 49
  Bishop Hopkins controverts 40
  Boon to backsliders . . 102
  Born of Dualism 41
  Breeds infidels and Pharisees 42

Page.

  Calvinists liable to . . . 86
  Characterised by Robt.
    Hall 348-52
  Cloaks immorality . . . 28
  Confounds Christ's and
    Edenic law 44
  Consistently expressed . 34
  Corollary of the "Decrees" 46
  Creed of 35
  Crisp well expressed . . 48
  Disastrousness of . . . 95-6
  Disinfects lechery . . . 146
  Dotes on law-less-ness 107-11
  Drops Calvinistic terms . 130
  Due to one-sided preaching 43
  Duplicity of 94
  Epidemic 349
  Fletcher discusses . 30-1, 50-1
  Formerly called Ana-baptists 45
  History of 37ff
  Hymns of . . . 96 : 107 : 113
  Imputes Christ's obedience 39
  In Luther's time 45

INDEX TO SUBJECTS AND NAMES.

	Page.
In Paul's day	38
Insures eternal life	143–4
Modern teachers of	143
Named by Luther	38
On Faith	100–1
On New Birth	116–7
Pharisaic	351
Relation to Calvinism	39
Sample expressions of	19
Sample of Conversion	104
Sin "in" and "on" the soul	105
Stated by Crisp	138–42
Substituted for religion	350f
Teaches imputed holiness	148–50
Imputed righteousness	32
Limited atonement	130
"Once in grace, always"	71
Taught by popular Evangelists	27
Universalism a species of,	41
Voids moral responsibility	143
Wesley characterizes and defines	38, 120, 354
Guards against	87
Atonement, truly described,	124
"Brethren's" view of	121
Augustine, on interpreting Scripture	118
Baxter, general and personal righteousness	92–3
Believers, first judged	277
Sins of, imaginary	89
"Two-roomed"	77

	Page.
Bengel, how far Wesley followed	273–4
Not a modern prem.	241
On pseudo-chiliasts	241
World's conversion before Advent	262
Bickersteth, antiquates the N. T.	232
Bishop transfers guilt to Christ	127
View of atonement met,	121–30
"Bishop who swore as a Lord"	63
"Branches," can they be cut off?	156
Brooks, J. H., Millennial Chart of	223
Minifies believers' sins	89
Teachings of, in a nutshell	352f
View of the Gospel's aim,	220
Character unimputable	154
Children of God, temptable and peccable	134–5
Chiliasm (see also P. B. Eschat: Mill)	272
"Christ a gigantic sinner"	125
"Christ holy for us"	90
Christ, his bodily return inevitable	232
Made "sin" or "sin-offering"	125
Why his return delayed	263
"Without sin"	341f
Christian perfection	94
Christians, sleeping	180
Churches, disesteemed	6
"delusions"	15

INDEX TO SUBJECTS AND NAMES.

"Comings" and "Coming" of Christ.
After the renovation . . 261
At Pentecost 301
By the Holy Spirit . . 306, 342
Dark side to 299, 306
Jamieson, Fausett and Brown on . . 285, 309, 311
Judicial and with power . 323
Not bodily 322
Manner of . . . 290, 318, 322
Many 283
Marks of 302, 310
Millen. like many others . 326
Not that of Ac. 1. 11 . . 325f
With power, not bodily 303–4
Not to save, but to condemn 264
Punitive side of 301
Spiritual and judicial . . 285
Sundry, 288f, 293, 296, 307–8, 314
Two sides to 290
Conditional life 132
Corporealists, makeshifts of 323
Cremer, "In Christ or the Lord" 156
Crisp, rankly states Antinomianism 138–42

Darby, Abolishes the ministry 11–2
Antagonized Wesleyanism 9
Avowed "unconditional election" 131
Influence in France . . 13
Labor in Switzerland . . 8

Leaves Church of England 6
"Liberality" of 10
On "the old man" . . . 60
Publications of . . . 9, 11
Sketch of . . . 5–20, 53–60
Strange statement by . . 58
Uses faulty text 158
View of judgment . . . 185

Earth, inhabited after destruction by fire . . 277
Epiphany 296
Evil of good works 47

Faith, attested by works . 29
Faith of depair 281
Figurative language, 277, 283–4, 305, 312, 316, 319, 325
Fletcher, on Antin. contradictions 152
Death the Sanctifier . . 106
Feeling 102
Sonship of God 134
Terms "sheep and goats" 137
Flesh, Biblical use of term 114–5
Foolish Virgins, saved or lost? 276

Gordon, lauds election . 215–6
Gospel, design of . . . 276–7
Only for the Bride . . 258–9
Writer's view of 23
Guilt not transferable . 126–8

Hall, Dr. Robt., on Antinomianism 348–52

"His Presence" 287
Holiness identified with
 Justification 17
Hopkins, paradox on belief
 and works 93
Hymenaeus 133

Imbrie, ignores Free
 Will 198-200
 Universalist utterance of, 197
Imputed holiness a pagan
 fiction 160
Imputed righteousness and
 holiness distinguished
 149-51
"In Christ," misapplication
 of phrase 151-3
 Pauline, sense of . . . 154-61
 Subjective and objective
 force of 159
 True meaning of phrase . 118
"Incorporation," danger-
 ous 95
Irenæus, on wine in the
 Millen. 209

J. R. C., Allegorizing inter-
 pretations 74
James, to Antin. of his day, 113
Jesus, holy in our stead . . 40
Joel's language fulfilled in
 Peter's day 213
Judgment, believers escape, 277
 Day of 333
 But one 277
 Universality of 333
Jukes, Andrew, an allego-
 rizer 75

Justification, not affected
 by sin 17
Justin, admission of, as to
 second coming . . . 331

Last days, began with In-
 carnation 340
 The Gospel dispensation . 341
Law, a sin to keep it . . . 58
 Our rule of life 348
 Sense in which believers
 free from 107-11
Leaven, misinterpretation
 of 73
Lee, Jesse 355
Literalism, difficulties of,
 204-14, 292
Luther, unguarded 123

McDonald, Wm., Introduc-
 tion by 5ff
McIntosh (C. H. M.), quoted
 16, 80-1
 Almost plenarily inspired 74
 Helplessness of Holy
 Spirit 60
 Licentiousness affects not
 standing with God . 146
 Rank and approved
 teacher of Antin. . 143-4
McNeile, antiquates the
 N. T. 233
Meyer, on conversion of
 Jews 258-9
 Quoted 155, 261
Moody, D. L., alluded to . 193
 A Premillenarian . . . 56

INDEX TO SUBJECTS AND NAMES. 367

Instructed by Plymouth
   Brethren 55
Müller, George, a schismatic "Brother" . . . 14
Müller, Julius, meaning of
   "flesh" 115

Neander, Church a part of
   the Kingdom 250
Noah's Ark, teaches perseverance of saints . . 75

Owen, quoted 242

Pagans, probation of . . . 175
"Paid it all," in what sense 111
Papias, on millennial
   abundance 208
Parable, net and pounds . 333f
   Wheat and tares 336f
Parsons, H. M., error as to
   Leaven 249
   Gentiles not redeemed . 218f
Paul, on works 114
Pearson, on creed, and return of Christ . . . 188
Pessimism, characteristic of
   Prem. 243
Phineas 133
Plymouth Brethren, -ism.
   American exponents of . 57
   Argument analyzed . . 65–8
   Refuted 82–4
   Checked in England . . 8
   Chiefly proselytize . . . 20
   Christian experience portrayed 18

Church, is not the Kingdom 246
Claim Moody 55
Close communionists . . 54
Commercial atonement of 58f
Confound Adamic and
   Christian law . . . 93
Conscience and consciousness of sin . . 81
Death the Sanctifier . . 61
Deny "Entire Sanctification" 105
Disintegrating influence
   of 57
Dissensions among . . . 57
Divisions among . . . 12–4
Duality life-long 64
Duplicity as to creeds . . 20
Eschatology of . . . 162ff
   Absurdities and perils
     of 244f
   Built on symbolic language 235
   Comforting security . . 180
   Conversions during the
     Millen. 166
   Deny general judgment, 183
   Disastrousness of . . . 265
   Earth during saints' absence 165
   Enervating 265
   Exegesis of Rev. xx. refuted 237–45
   Founded on Calvinistic
     election 214
   Furnishes Jews an excuse 252–5
   Gospel minified . 166–8, 196

	Page.
Grossly materialistic	191
"In Christ," interpretation of	181
Inconsistencies of	206f
Insults the Holy Spirit,	169
Jewish errors repeated in	251
Jews reign in the Millen.	166
Multiply resurrections	230
Judgment days	229
Nations, not individuals, judged	167
New heavens and new earth	168
Offices for the saints	164f
Parable of mustard seed	173
Perverts parable of leaven	170
Probation closed with Adam	175
Radical error of	183
"Rapture of the Saints," secret	163
Saints never in the judgment	179
Sophistries of	174
Speculation fostered by	169
Spirit's work minified	168
Substitutes force for persuasion	201
Teaches a localizing of Christianity	210f
Those "In Christ" uncondemnable	177
Two future Advents	162
Wicked dead judged	168
Works, not persons, judged	182
Evils of teachings	21
Exegesis of	70f
From Plymouth, Eng.	7
General judgment denied	87
Great tract distributers	55
Hate Wesleyan Christian perfection	78
How Universalism avoided	60
In a nut-shell	51, 352
Literalizes figurative language	73
Moral distinctions obliterated	90
Safeguards discarded	85
New birth, as taught by	15
Origin of	5
Other names of	5
Prefer name of "Brethren"	7
Rank Pessimists	169
Santification, contradictory idea of	79
Shibboleth of meetings	12
Sketch of	52ff
Spurious "perfection" of	26
Strictest Antinomians	15
Sympathisers with	56
Twin brambles	9
Tyng's sympathy with	56
Uncritical scholarship of	72
Use and abuse of the Bible	55
Wresters of the Scripture	64
Poetry, to be read by poetical canons	324
Popular Evangelists teach Antin.	27

INDEX TO SUBJECTS AND NAMES.

Premillennialists, -ism.
Alford on 280
Ancient 279
Burton 280f
Dionysius 281
Early, why it declined . 280
Eusebius 280
Extravagances of . . . 278
Favored by heretics . . 280
Ignored by early church . 280
Jamieson and Faussett . 280
Jewish Chiliasm of . . . 280
Justin 280
Makeshifts of 345f
Milman 280
Modern, essential error of 279
  Its claims in brief . . 275–7
  Unscripturalness of . . 282
Mosheim 280
Neander 280
Rejected by all creeds and
  confessions 187
Schlegel 280
Wesley, falsely claimed
  as 271–4
  Utterly negatives its es-
  sence 271–81
Prophetic conference, Cal-
  vinist complexion of . 195
Central idea of 194
Of 1878 and 1886 275
Universalism of 197

Repentance, demanded of
  sinners 98
"Restitution of all things," 260
Resurrection, of saints only,
  or all? 277

Return of Jews, unknown
  to Paul 186
Return of Christ, Creeds
  thereon 188–90
  Why delayed 202
Revelation, Book of, Schools
  of interpreters of . . 236

Saints, "Rapture of," secret 276
Sandeman, Epitaph of . . 355
Satan loosed 167
Sears, effect of atonement . 120
Second Advent, after or
  before the Millen.? . 275
Converts not 327f
Ends the earth . . . 343–5
  Mediatorial kingdom . 338
  Mortality 329f
  Probation 332–7
Enlarges probation . . . 276
Judgment for all immedi-
  ately follows 274
Redemptive powers cease
  at 339ff
To convert, or to judge,
  the world? . . . 275–6
"Sheep becoming a goat?" 137
Simpson, A. B., advocate of
  modern Prem. . . . 275
Sin, harmless in believers 35
"In" us and "on" us . 35
"Sinful flesh" and body per-
  petually confounded . 69
Sinning "in Christ" . . . 28
Smith, J. D., permanence of
  sin 62
"State" and "standing,"
    69, 79, 81, 145

	Page.
"Standing" is independent of "State"	153
Taylor, D. T., concession of	313
Bishop, found Antin. in India	160
"Temporal kingdom" expected, but "a dream"	276
"The kingdom," future, or present?	276
Set up after Second Advent	275
"Thousand Years"	321
Trench, on parable of leaven	249
Tyreman, misrepresents Wesley	271–3
Weiss, interpretation mentioned	115

	Page.
Wesley, John, not a modern Premillen.	241
On feeling	108
Whedon, D. A., Was Christ "punished"?	129
Whedon, D. D., quoted	256
On generation and regeneration	115
Whitefield, On a religion without feeling	102
Whittle, Maj., Allegorizing interpreter	74
Works, set before Jews	111f
World's conversion, before, not by, Advent	258–62
Y. M. C. A., infected with Antinom.	27
Sample of theology	124